BUTTERFLIES AND FEATHERS

Ann Annis

authorHOUSE®

AuthorHouse™ UK Ltd.
500 Avebury Boulevard
Central Milton Keynes, MK9 2BE
www.authorhouse.co.uk
Phone: 08001974150

© 2011. Ann Annis. All rights reserved

No part of this book may be reproduced, stored in a retrieval system, or transmitted by any means without the written permission of the author.

First published by AuthorHouse   02/5/2011

ISBN: 978-1-4567-7454-7

Any people depicted in stock imagery provided by Thinkstock are models, and such images are being used for illustrative purposes only. Certain stock imagery © Thinkstock.

This book is printed on acid-free paper.

Because of the dynamic nature of the Internet, any web addresses or links contained in this book may have changed since publication and may no longer be valid. The views expressed in this work are solely those of the author and do not necessarily reflect the views of the publisher, and the publisher hereby disclaims any responsibility for them.

Once a Fusilier, Always a Fusilier

I remember walking through old run down cemeteries, many, many times and long before our son died. Plots long neglected, weathered stones, the names barely recognizable and shriveled flowers of past family visits. I think to myself that these people once had a life, these lost ones once held an identity, and they were loved. Had they accomplished what they strived to do in life? Now they are alone and forgotten, many a distant memory.

When we lost Simon, I knew that I would persevere to do all I could to keep his memory alive, to keep his name prominent. So, by writing this book, I hope that in twenty or fifty years from now, someone may find and read it, then one way or another my boy will be there somewhere in someone's thoughts.

This book has been the hardest challenge I have ever had to deal with. I started writing it eight months after Simon was lost to us. It reveals the emotions I went through, the memories I thought about each day, and this is something I needed to do, and finish. I had much input from people who knew Simon and I would like to thank them all, especially my husband Peter. But most of all, I would like to thank the person who gave me all these special remarkable memories,

"Mummies Little Soldier".
My son, Simon.

Contents

A Hero is born	1
Dobber	5
Holidays and sandy boats	9
Simon Invades France	12
Simons Menagerie	16
Fishing Expeditions	20
Household Games	23
Highschool Days	27
Friends	34
Simons career decisions	37
Simon's home life	43
Mummies little soldier	47
The proudest day of my life	51
Overseas	55
Coming of age	62
Christmas 2008	65
2009	70
Rest and relaxation	76
Death Valley, Sangin	83
Repatriation	100
Simon's final resting place	105
Butterflies and feathers	123
The Inquest	130
Letter from Gordon Brown	133
Life without Simon 2010	136

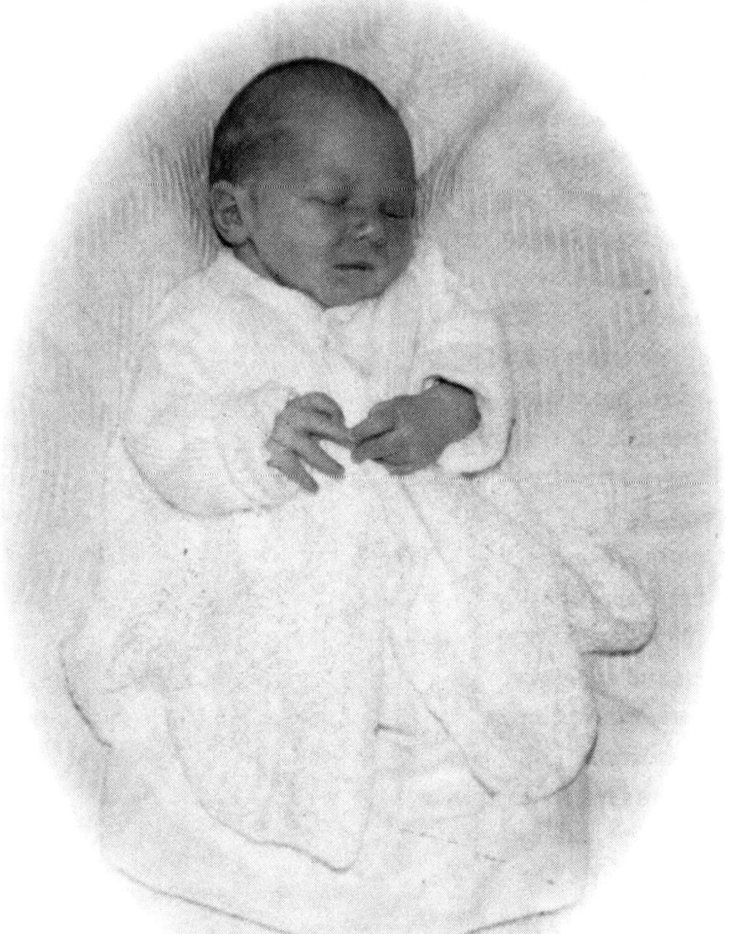

A Hero is born

I do not pretend to be a professional author. I am just an ordinary mum doing ordinary things. I am writing this story about my son. My son, Simon Annis, was only twenty two years old when he died. He wasn't a film star, a celebrity, or even a multimillionaire. He was a normal, cheeky, fun loving Salford boy.

Tragically on the 16th August 2009, 25225641 Fusilier Simon Annis was killed by an I.E.D (Improvised Explosive Device). In a word, bomb. He died for Queen and Country and that's what they told us. He died a week to the day of his 22nd birthday. His dad Peter and I were there to welcome him into this world, but sadly we couldn't be there to guide him out of it. That's one task my brave little man had to do all by himself. He was a mummy's boy and that was the one thing he wouldn't have wanted to do without me.

On the 9th August 1987, my middle child was born, all six pound and nine ounces of him. He was lighter than his two siblings and his birth was a breeze really compared to the other two. It's as if he came into this world smiling, laid back, just glad to be here. He looked so comical with his scrawny long legs and his tufts of soft brown hair just around the sides, like a little old man. He would scratch away at his face so hard it sometimes bled, so the scratch mitts were part of him for weeks. He soon altered, taking on the looks of a cute, cuddly little baby, with a mop of thick blonde hair and eyes so blue. Within five hours of giving birth I was home with Simon in my arms, doing the vacuuming. He stayed in my arms for many years, wanting cuddles and lots of love. He was to be that perfect angel child, not demanding and very content, always happy and smiling.

When I was six weeks pregnant with Simon, I fell ill. A searing pain ripped through my stomach. Pete called the doctor out and he warned me that I could lose my baby. I was told to rest but I was petrified as I stroked my stomach. "You're not going anywhere", I told this new life growing inside me. After two days that pain subsided and my baby was safe. It was two years later that my appendix ruptured. It was the same pain I had felt whilst carrying Simon. I didn't't't realize how close I came to losing him, and I thank God I had him for a precious twenty two years.

When he was nine months old I reluctantly bought a play pen for him. It would come in useful. Stuart, his elder brother, was then four years old and the pair needed watching constantly. If he didn't take to it, I would return it, I thought. But to my delight he absolutely loved it and he would actually cry if I tried to take him out. This was his private safe haven. Simon demonstrated from such a young age how content and happy he was in his own company. Stuart was a very demanding child and Natalie, his little sister, was typically girly in every way. Stuart and Natalie were so much alike in many ways. They were always coming forward with a problem or a worry and were both very strong minded and loud children, yet Simon was different. I love all my children equally, but Simon had a grace about him. I can't pinpoint it, but he was different, special.

As a toddler he would sit happily in his chair and play with Tupperware bowls, with wooden pegs inside. He would take out the pegs; bash the tubs with the wooden spoon, always chattering to himself. I bet he told many a tale in his own baby language. I would have loved nothing more than to be able to translate what he was saying. I gathered that this was his pleasant laid back personality set in place from a very young age.

Simon had a pacifier, it was his pram blanket. He carried it everywhere. It was a pale yellow knitted blanket and this grubby tatty blanket went everywhere he went. He clung to it and one day while he was in his buggy, he dropped it. It was twenty minutes later that he realized and I had to retrace our steps to find it. When we eventually found it, dirty and wet, he clung to it and sat by the washing machine watching for the cycle to end. I had to cut bits off it to make it smaller and as he got older I got it to the size of a handkerchief. He owned three dummies which he called dowdies. He didn't have them in the day but in the morning he would come downstairs and hide them behind a certain picture frame and just before bed he would retrieve them.

By the age of three, Simon was offered a place in nursery. Stuart had taken to it fairly well but I honestly thought we would have had problems with

Simon but he was ok if he had the constant companionship of his teachers. He was a young three, only just having had his third birthday and already in school. He couldn't get the hang of talking yet. He had a slight lisp so communication was not his best asset but it made him all the cuter. When people heard him trying to talk their response was "Aw isn't he so cute!" They would then pinch his little cheeks. Simon had an infectious giggle and he had that cheeky giggle always, even into adulthood.

By infant school he had matured a little and started to mix with the other children but still preferred the teacher's company. Simon had perfected the perfect bottom lip, so adorable it was, it would build up, slowly, slowly, then there it was. I used to tell him that I could balance a tea cup on it. This would make him run into my arms, clutching on to me so tight I could feel his little nails pinching my skin. Sobbing uncontrollably, he looked so helpless, poor tiny little mite.

He had been a perfect baby. He crawled early and walked just before he was eleven months old. When he cut his first tooth his little cheeks glowed so red and were so hot to touch, he suffered so much but he rarely cried. He sailed through the "terrible two's" stage, with no tantrums. It was a pleasure to have such a contented child.

Ann Annis

Simon's much loved play pen

Cornish Pasties

Dobber

Simon was four years and nine months old when he acquired the nickname "Dobber", this remained with him for the rest of his short life. I was attending a maypole event at the boys Infant School and I took Natalie, who was then fourteen months old, along to watch the boys. It was a beautiful, hot, May afternoon and the boys worked hard to master the maypole. We watched them happily hop and dance around the maypole with the music ringing out, so sweet and innocent they both looked, I took pictures thinking these are the type of pictures their girlfriends will get to see many years from now.

When they finished their exhausting exercise they were handed an ice-cream as a treat. The children eagerly waited in line for their reward. In an instant Natalie spotted this delicious treat and quickly toddled over to Simon, who now had received his. My cheeky daughter's lips were chomping together in anticipation and with arms outstretched she looked up at Simon, her lips chomping faster and faster. "Dobber, Dobber "she cried stamping her feet. He looked down at her and casually offered her his ice cream. Because he responded to that name that day, it stuck with her always. I haven't a clue how the name Simon became "Dobber" but from that day on it was to be his second permanent name.

The three children grew extremely close, played together happily with very few quarrels and fortunately no sibling fighting We were lucky, we strived to bring up our children right, with morals, respect and an understanding of life and its many pitfalls. Simon struggled through infant school and he often got frustrated with the work. He found it hard, but he got there in the end. His true personality and many qualities shone through, still that laid back happy boy. During the summer days he would happily play in the garden. Ants, he loved the things. The garden would resemble that of a mole outbreak after a day of Simons play. He would collect ants by the hundreds in any container available. I remember hunting in the cupboards, finding anything of use for him, in the end having to nip to the shop to purchase cartons of Pringles. When empty these were perfect for his little friends. "Hmm", I wondered sometimes did he really need the cartons or was it a cunning rouse to get the crisps for himself.

One day after looking tirelessly for ants there seemed to be a shortage in the garden, perhaps they grew wise as not to enter when Simon was on the loose, so he asked our next door neighbors Lynne and Dennis to look for ants in their garden. I was peeping out of the kitchen window finding it all amusing. Simon was on his tiptoes against their fence, impatiently waiting for the rewards from their garden and for me watching a middle aged couple tirelessly lifting stones and plant pots so as not to disappoint him was the highlight of my day. Then he would set himself to work, digging tunnels and mud homes for these unfortunate creatures, making pathways and swimming pools out of sunken yogurt pots. Poor things, they didn't like the pool much, but Simon was boss and they swam. When he had to call it a day, tea and bath calling, he left all kinds of food out from the kitchen cupboard without me knowing, always returning the next morning to care for his little wards.

Next came the Action Men, he loved these. It was all-out war when Barbie met Action Man. Natalie was not amused as he would wrestle them both and I would see Barbie being launched up one of our large conifers. All in all, I could say he had a fascinating imagination. In the summer, we had paddling pools in the garden, I loved this myself but this meant that there was no room for the children as Pete and I sat in them to cool down with a glass of cold wine. The pool wasn't one of the large ones you see today; we had a small one. They did get in eventually but not until Pete had delighted in winding them up. Simon enjoyed the pool, but as strange as it was, the home bath was a no go area for him. It would often take two of us to hold him in there. Pete held, I scrubbed, and you could hear his tantrum all the way down the street. I haven't a clue where this fear originated from. I look back and still have no idea.

Butterflies and Feathers

Simons Childhood

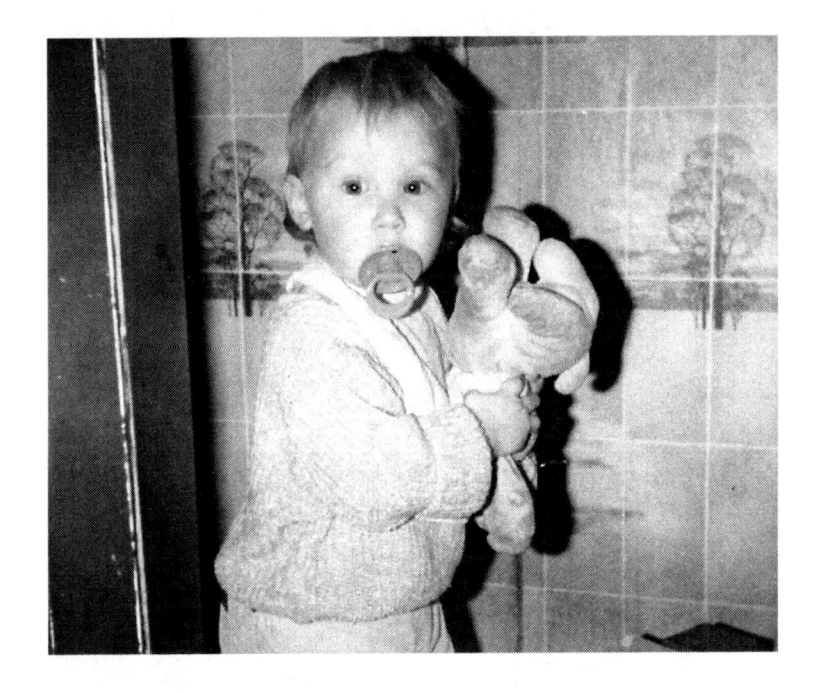

Ann Annis

Holidays and sandy boats

When our children were small, we took them on holiday to St Ives in Cornwall. It was somewhere familiar with Pete, as he had spent many holidays there as a child, with his large family and I also liked the place. One day I would move there, I would day dream, one day. We must have held the record for the family who could eat the most Cornish pasties in a week. I have a photo of the three children sitting side by side on a door step each holding a pasty, the pasties being bigger than they were. We ate them constantly, breakfast, dinner and tea, not very nutritious but hey we were on our holidays.

There was plenty to do and one of our favourite pastimes was crab fishing. We used fishing line with bacon tied to the end and when one of the children caught one, they would gleefully celebrate and triumph over their catch. We weren't very lucky with weather that year. It was dull and gloomy which can put a dampener on any holiday, so when the sun made a rare appearance we eagerly packed beach towels and a picnic and off the Annis crowd went. The beach was enormous, the white sands stretched as far as the eye could see, with large sand dunes meeting the beach. It was a busy day, children amusing themselves making sand castles. Frisbees and kites filled the clear blue sky, it was beautiful, no need to travel abroad, not when it's like this I thought, perfect.

We walked towards the water's edge and hastily kicked off our shoes and strolled along letting cool salt sea water splash our now hot feet. Pete stopped and announced, "Right, you lot who's coming in" and that was it, with no warning or explanation Simon started to run. Pete and I stood arms crossed, watching, "he will be back in a minute" Pete said. We shouted after him, he didn't even look back, his eyes transfixed on the route ahead, on the beach, as far away from water as possible. When Pete realized that this little lad was on a mission, he started chase. Simon made a lot of distance, more than we thought and Pete was exhausted when he arrived back to us with Simon dangling under one arm, so we didn't get to swim that year. It would be a few years later when we eventually gave it another try.

Simon was older now and the part of his life where he feared water had gone. Here was my new water baby. We had a lovely time, it was perfect. I would sit on my beach towel reading and watching Pete regressing back to his childhood as he and the boys, armed with plastic spades, began to dig into the sand. Their mission was to dig out a boat. With architect Pete overlooking the workers, they started to dig out this boat. They made it quite close to the oncoming tide, it was the biggest sand boat I have ever seen and thinking about that, it was the first sand boat I had ever seen. This was no normal boat as it came with seats inside. They all stood and admired their accomplished artwork, after a mad hour of frantic digging, hooray, there it was, perfect. Now the point to all of this was, when the tide came in, the boat had to be saved, so with all the children seated and dad at the helm, the adventure would begin. Then the children anxiously waited for the tide to inch closer, the look of concentration and worry in their eyes told me this was for real. As the tide now reached the boat, the cries of panic and excitement echoed the beach as the Annis family refused to let the boat be taken by the sea. Stuart and Simon were frantically propping up the sides with replacement sand, little legs running round to strengthen the weakening front, buckets filled and given to dad to reinforce the interior. Only when there was no hope and the tide too strong they knew that they were sadly defeated. If I could imagine myself as a child again, I would imagine that this was a true adventure, even if it lasted just a short time.

Before returning home, we gave our children a special treat, a trip on the fishing boat to catch mackerel. Natalie wasn't too happy, she wasn't a sea lover but she came along regardless. We were driven out to sea not too far but far enough to see the distant shore. Pete and I hadn't done this before either. The crew in charge gave us rods and these rods had at least ten hooks dangling all the way down the line. How hard could it be I thought? We lowered our lines and within minutes we were lifting them up and out of the water, it was fun, we caught dozens of mackerel. Simon on the other hand had to do things differently from everyone else. He lowered his line and immediately brought it back up; he had caught fish but not full live tasty fresh mackerel as he hoped. One hook had the remains of a fishes jaw, another with a piece of tail, and the last one had a fin attached. He had all his fish, but not necessarily in the right order. He had struck too hard on his rod.

We had some good times on that holiday and it was one that stuck in the children's minds for years after. I won't forget that fishing trip either, although we were out in the middle of the sea, it was on me that the seagull decided to drop a present, the children thought this hilarious.

Simon Invades France

We had our first family holiday abroad when Natalie was four, Simon seven and Stuart ten. A good deal came up that we could not resist. Three weeks for the price of two with Euro camp in France. What an adventure, we would get to travel on a ferry for the first time. "Wow" the children said when we approached the port. The journey was notably rocky and giving the children scrambled egg for lunch was probably a bad idea. Out came the travel sickness pills which I don't think helped the matter as they made us all drowsy. Simon was particularly bad, he was very pale, and so we sat the whole journey outside in the seating area to get fresh air into him.

We arrived in Calais, ahead of us a further six hour journey to our destination and with the children constantly asking "are we nearly there yet" it felt much longer. We finally arrived at the French campsite where the large family tent was erected and waiting for us. As Pete and I steadily unpacked our cases and made up beds, the children set about investigating this new and exciting place. It was a very beautiful part of France and the camp site was amid a large oak filled forest and very peaceful for the time of year in June. We went shopping for food and essentials then a chance to relax, sitting outside with a BBQ, blessed by the nice warm weather, just what we needed after a long hard journey. Simon was already in a digging frenzy, digging holes near the back of the tent. I don't know what his aim was but he was content. We were tired and the children were shattered so we had an early night in readiness for the next day, a nice fresh early start is what we all needed. And I did get that early start, three am, I awoke in the pitch black of the night to the sounds of scurrying under my bed. I shot up, listened, no it wasn't my imagination, there were mice under our bed.

"Oh my God" I shouted, Pete felt for the torch. As the torch flicked on we saw the mice separate in all directions, I cringed, and that night I tried to stay awake with the torch shining by my side. The next morning we awoke to another beautiful warm day, Pete fetched water for a nice cup of tea. While outside he noticed that Simon, it had to be him, had pushed BBQ food down holes he had found near the edges of the tent. Surprise, surprise, the edges that were adjacent to our bedroom, probably a coincidence I thought or did our little animal lover encourage them in.

The last straw was the next morning when we awoke to see our very large family chocolate cake, bought the day before, being virtually stolen from our tent. We couldn't see the cake, it was a seething mass of black scurrying ants, big ants, my eyes narrowed as I looked accusingly at Simon and yes more evidence of left over BBQ food which had been put in homemade ant houses, actually inside the tent's edges. That was it for me, we upgraded to a caravan, more expense, but it didn't't stop there. Believe it or not, things did get worse.

On the third day, I noticed Simon scratching his head frantically. After I examined his scalp I was horrified to find he had brought head lice with him. I couldn't believe this was happening; now he was to start a nit epidemic in France. Worse still he had been playing with a little lad, whose family we had met only that morning, he couldn't have caught them from this other youngster, Simon was crawling with them. With children in tow, Pete and I went in search of the nearest large town. Stuart and Natalie kept their distance from Simon as if he were a leper. There we found a chemist. Simon was not fazed one bit, not a care in the world. Upon entering a very crowded chemist, we waited in line to be dealt with. I could see one of Simon's little pests at the end of a tuft of hair, I flicked at it quickly.

Our turn at last and we tried to explain to the assistant that we needed head lice treatment but having no French language skills, it was impossible. After five minutes of hopeless interaction the assistant suddenly looked horrified and retreated to the back of the shop. Another man came through quickly and to Pete's and my utter embarrassment announced to the whole shop, "you have lice". He was saying this while scratching all of his body. I knew he thought we had body lice and I felt my face burn red. All the eyes in the shop were on us, waiting on a reply. "No, no" I quickly said pointing to Simon's head while making scratching gestures. "Ha" he said and gave me a tin of head lice lotion. We were out of that shop so quickly that the children's feet didn't touch the floor.

Just going off this subject altogether for a moment, I feel the need to tell you this. As I am writing this, I am crying because the song I adopted for Simon has just come on the radio, "Arms of an Angel" by Sarah McLachlan. If you listen to this beautiful song you will understand.

We arrived back at the tent within the hour and quickly sat Simon down with a towel over his shoulders. We couldn't understand the French instructions on the lotion, so we put it all on him; it came out as foam and smothered his tiny head. He screeched and with his eyes now watering, his little face went a very strange deep red colour. He resembled one of those "Umpa lumpas" out of the film "Charlie and the Chocolate Factory". I rushed him to the nearest shower block to wash it off; it worked fantastic, not a head louse in sight. I was so impressed that I went back and bought two more tins to take home. After our crazy three days of mice, ants and nits, we had an absolutely fantastic time. The weather remained nice and warm, and the children enjoyed every minute of it.

Shortly after this holiday I remember sitting Simon down and sternly telling him that putting things up his nose and eating anything that wasn't food, was not acceptable. He would chew on anything that came to hand, wallpaper, newspaper, and bits of broken toys. He was worse than a chewing puppy. One instance I remember, he was sitting on the toilet and had been there a long time, but then again he often was, messing about with Pete's razor and aftershaves.

He started shouting "Mum, mum" he was crying. So, Pete ran upstairs and all I could hear downstairs was "Arggh dad that hurts" with Pete replying, "sit still". I know this is disgusting, but I have to mention it, because this was one of the many things we had to endure with Simon. Simon had eaten a large piece of string and what goes in must come out, and this was one of those times that the string came out. Poor Pete had to remove it from Simon's back end. But still, it didn't teach him and he continued to eat anything in his way.

Then there was the ball up his nose. He had found a little yellow plastic ball and thought the place for this was up his nose. Sadly that is where it ended up. He casually strolled over to me "look" he said, lifting his chin and pointing to his nose. Upon further inspection I could just make out a yellow object pushed way up in his nostril. "Simon" I shouted "what now?!" I was fuming, did this child never learn. I didn't know what to do, I was scared that if he sniffed up it would lodge at the back of his throat "Breath through your mouth, don't sniff up" I said, panicking. He wandered about the house with his mouth open wide, resisting the urge to sniff. Pete was working nearby, he was very busy, but what could I do. I put Simon in the car and drove quickly to find him. As we approached his place of work, Pete spotted the car and met us. I told him what Simon had done; "come here" Pete said to Simon and lifted his chin up, took a look at the offending object and told him "blow your nose, hard". With one snort, the ball came free, as easy as that. I felt a bit stupid, why didn't't I do that, I wondered. Simon wanted his ball back, not a chance I told him "get in the car". Another frustrating day with Simon!

Simons Menagerie

The Annis family had an array of wildlife, either situated in the home or in the garden. Apart from the usual ants and slugs, we had fish and many dogs, one we still have today. This one was Simon's playmate and favourite. He is a thirteen year old Yorkshire terrier named Mojo so named after the song "Mojo Rising" by Peter's favourite band, "The Doors". Then there was Fiver, our cute brown lop eared rabbit, named after his purchase price. This rabbit was an oddity. He could actually play good football. Simon would try and score past Fiver into the make shift goal, but Fiver always managed to take the ball off Simon, much to his delight. Simon would play with Fiver for hours on end. Sadly he vanished after the local fox visited our garden one night. The next day we searched everywhere for him and we told Simon he had escaped to be with his friends in the wild. Pete knew this was untrue because earlier that day he had found poor Fiver's little tail on the lawn, so sadly we knew of his demise.

Then along came Henry, the extraordinary white duck. We rescued him at a very young age; he was the worst bad tempered duck I had ever come across. Every morning, upon release from his pen, he would take up guard in the middle of the lawn, patiently waiting for unsuspecting sparrows to land. When they did he would be in hot pursuit of them, angrily quacking with wings shaking violently to chase them off from his territory. Endlessly he would do this from one end of the garden to the other," totally obsessive", I used to say, but when he was around Simon he was quite the opposite. He waddled after him everywhere. One boy and his duck. We had the company of Henry for two years and he was beginning to be a handful. He would not go back in his pen at night and Pete would chase him everywhere. Henry made sure that Pete was shattered by the end of it all. The only way for Pete, to grab him, was to chase him into the house where Henry took refuge behind the TV. I would grumble as I cleaned up the droppings that Henry thoughtfully left behind. We let Henry go free on a nearby estate. Our beautiful fat white duck didn't deserve to be denied the chance of freedom.

Butterflies and Feathers

Arthur, another lop eared rabbit, was very special to us and we actually managed to keep him from the clutches of the resident fox clan. Arthur's name was chosen by the children, we had him for a good three years. He couldn't play football or anything else like our other exocentric pets, but was just plain old lovable Arthur. Age eventually took its toll on him. He developed an abscess near his ear, and endless visits to the vet were required, medication was administered daily. Arthur grew weak. When winter set in, Arthur was too frail to remain outside, so we brought him and his cage indoors. We set it up in an unused bedroom, where he stayed in the warmth of the home. He was rapidly growing weaker but the children refused to give him up. Simon sat with Arthur many nights soothingly stroking and chatting to him. Late one winter's night, Pete came down after visiting Arthur and told us that Arthur was blind. I went to see and it broke my heart. I spoke to Arthur and I could tell he couldn't see me, he was just following the sound of my voice. He crept very slowly towards me and I knew then this could not go on. I told the children that it was unacceptable and very cruel to let Arthur carry on with so much pain. They tearfully agreed. In his younger days, Pete worked voluntarily with a game keeper so he wasn't fazed by what he was about to do. Quickly and painlessly, as I waited silently downstairs with the children, Pete carried out the terrible task. The children didn't speak to Pete for hours afterwards. Even though we discussed what needed to be done, Pete bore the brunt of their anguish.

We then bought Simon a hamster and he named him Biff. He took really good care of Biff; in fact he cared for him too well. I'm not sure whether chips and burger was a good staple diet for a hamster! Biff became too fat, he managed to squeeze into his play tube, then died. We had to bury him in his tube. Poor Simon dug a hole for him in the garden; we all stood silently for yet another pet funeral. Two days later Simon asked "Can I have another hamster", I sternly answered "No".

On Simon's approach to his sixteenth birthday he insisted that it was a parrot he wanted. Maybe now that he was a little more mature, he would be able to cope with such a huge responsibility, how naive I was. I went along with Pete and Simon to the large local pet shop and after browsing the budgies and other small feathered creatures, we came across a large aviary. Inside, looking so cute was a baby African Grey parrot. Simon stood gazing at this bird, cooing and saying "who's a pretty boy then." He had managed to save half the money up himself, so I knew he was committed to the care of the bird. The total cost came to twelve hundred pounds with cage, food and accessories. Very expensive but I eventually gave in to his puppy dog eyes routine. Simon named him Bart after his favourite animation series the Simpsons. We bought all the books to hopefully give him advice on the best way to train Bart and we had him for two years.

We tried all we could to train Bart but he dominated the household. He was the ultimate bird from hell, he detested everyone but Natalie. This was Simon's pet but after the constant biting, Simon gave up on him and grew bored of the thing. When he was out of his cage he abused everyone, even the dog, who would cower in its presence. I was also petrified of Bart. I bought all the best fresh produce and toys to keep him from boredom but he repaid me by stripping the wallpaper and eating the curtains. We did manage to teach him a few words "Ouch" was his favourite, this he copied from me, whenever he bit me. He would also shout out his name in an American accent, "Bart, Bart".

It all got too much for me and in the end I was left in full custody of this juvenile delinquent. If we had company over, Bart would spitefully screech so loud it pierced our ears. I then had to push him and his cage into another room. He would then feel sorry for himself and all we could hear was, "Bart, good boy". This wasn't working, we basically didn't have a clue of how to care for him, and so I sent him packing to a good home where they had the experience and time to spend with him.

"No more pets "I told Simon and I meant it this time. Unfortunately we never did learn our lesson. Just before we got our normal, sensible, non-chewing Mojo, we had Zach, the mad lump of a Labrador. I remember many happy times of play in the garden. I was a tomboy mum, which helped because we had sons. We played rugby and football most nights on the lawn in the garden, the boys would tackle me, and then run for fear of a kick to their shins, we would get quite rough and wrestle Pete to the ground. He would then get up as if he were "Shrek," and shrug us all off.

One day I got a bee in my bonnet, I saw a black nine month old Labrador for sale. I wanted him, so I bought him, without thinking of the consequences. I bought an older dog thinking all the chewing stages were out of the way, how wrong I was. I should have realized when I went for him, as he was kept outside in a kennel, the yard was full of holes and large half eaten sticks covered the area. The instant I brought him home he disappeared to the back of the garden. I screamed when he ran back inside and plopped my large gold lion head fish down in front of me, where it wriggled gasping for breath and totally covered in mud. I quickly picked up this defenseless creature and gently washed him, miraculously he survived the ordeal. After nearly twelve months and hundreds upon hundreds of pounds spent, he had to go. I couldn't take any more. Why was it every pet we got turned out to be related to Freddy Krueger? I remember once we had a new kitchen carpet fitted, it looked lovely. I left Zach for an hour, on my return I was devastated to find he had eaten half of it so I went out and bought an anti-chew spray. The next morning we woke up to find he had eaten the spray bottle, along with the other half of the carpet. He wouldn't stop and was obliterating the home; he could not be left alone. I needed to go to Tesco so I took Zach along.

"Ha" I thought, you won't chew now. I only left him for a short time but on my return I cried as he had eaten most of my dash board, unfamiliar wires dangled from underneath. I was distraught, but now I smile when I remember Simon, sat on the back door step with his little shorts on, football socks rolled down, and his teenage mutant hero trainers on. Zach was sat next to him with legs to one side, his fat belly to the other, saliva dribbled from his huge mouth. He was refusing to eat his dinner as he knew there was medication hidden amongst it. Simon spoon fed him, he sat intently until the bowl was empty, then Simon took a tissue and wiped the dog's sloppy jowls. Simon loved this dog but he was another pet we couldn't't put up with and he went to live on a farm which was a place better suited to Zach.

After Zach, playing on the lawn was delayed as in the middle of it was a gaping wide 2ft x 2ft hole, where he had dug to bury one of his many sticks that he had torn off my conifers. I had an idea; we would get Astra Turf laid. When it came it looked perfect, no more muddy lawns, no more grass cuttings. I was so pleased with it and I became the laughing stock of the street when I started to Ewbank it every day.

Fishing Expeditions

Peter and I took up fishing, an interesting hobby, a way to relax amongst the beauty of nature and a chance to spend a little quality time together, except on the few occasions that we took the children along. On one of these occasions, we took them to a large beautiful lake which was local to us called Lymm Dam. The surroundings were breathtaking. With rods, chairs and picnics, in fact all but the kitchen sink, we set off. Although we were amateurs at the sport we didn't do too badly, however Pete didn't get the chance to fish as he was forever busy untangling the children's lines or climbing the overhead trees to rescue a float or two. Simon resembled "Huckleberry Fin" as he sat intently watching for the slightest movement of the float, getting bored if nothing happened within five minutes.

Simon had the habit of losing his grip whilst casting and launched his rod into the water. He got bored quite quickly and kept himself amused with the bowl of maggots. He and Natalie raced them against each over. When I was very young I also liked to fish and being a bit of a tomboy, I preferred football and fishing over clothes and dolls, so when I showed Simon how we used to keep the maggots warm in the winter he was horrified. "If you don't warm them up in the cold weather they won't wriggle" I said as I popped a maggot onto my tongue. They looked disgustedly at me.

As they often did Simon and Natalie wandered off, not too far as they knew their boundaries. They loved exploring this place as it wasn't just a lake; it was surrounded by lush thick shrubbery with perfect materials for making a den and hidey places. We could hear them playing and happy giggles rang out behind us. On one occasion Simon and Natalie came back with Simon rubbing his elbow and looking quite pale. He explained that whilst chasing Natalie he had fallen and hurt his elbow. Upon inspection I knew that this needed a hospital visit. In fact he had broken his elbow in the exact place that Pete had broken his as a child. To my annoyance the truth was unearthed years later, when I found out he had not broken it the way he said he had. There is a dangerous clay cliff at the Dam and he didn't need to be told that it was out of bounds. He fell down this cliff and concocted a tale to hide the truth and had sworn his sister to secrecy. We went back many times to the Dam and eventually Simon became confident and patient with the art of fishing, often going by himself in his teenage years, preferring his own company.

One summer's day Pete, Simon, Natalie and myself jumped into the car for a trip out to the countryside. On the journey we had to make an unexpected stop on one of the country lanes. Although the windows were closed and there was an unusual number of bluebottles in the car. When Pete opened the boot, there was an all-out explosion of bluebottles. The inside windows of the car were smothered and Natalie ran away screaming. Simon was hysterical with laughter; we had stupidly left a bait box full of maggots in the boot after fishing. In the hot weather they had hatched and dead flies covered the boot floor. Simon picked them out curiously scrutinizing each one. My skin crawled as there must have been thousands of these disgusting insects. It took quite a while before we could continue on our journey.

We went on family days out as often as we could, even if it was a walk in the countryside with a picnic or to Simon's most favourite place of all, Chester Zoo. Pete on the other hand dreaded this three times a year routine expedition to the zoo. He used to say, "Once you have been to the zoo, you see all there is to see". I suppose he was right but I too loved the place, so each time Pete was outvoted. On one of these visits Simon acquired three of his all-time favourite toys, a plastic dinosaur, a shark and a snake. He loved these toys and they went everywhere with him. Although he played with his Action Men he still preferred these three and I would watch him, deep in thought, sitting on the floor with crossed legs, hissing as the snake attacked the shark then growling when the dinosaur came to its defense, he kept these for many years although he ate the dinosaur's tail.

Another regular visit of ours was to Tatton Park, which is a large country estate. The children loved this place and we often went inside the big house, to experience how the Victorians lived. Although the children were only in their junior years they did genuinely find this very interesting and they would ask the stewards on duty many questions about the lives of our past ancestors.

Ann Annis

One hot sunny day Pete and I visited Tatton Park along with Simon and Natalie. They were older now and it was lovely to be out with the pair of them. Simon had a crazy idea; he wanted to do a three legged race. But there are four of us I informed him. "Ok, a four legged race then" he excitedly said, so we tied our ankles together using belts and socks. It was hilarious; we were totally oblivious to our surroundings and the strange glances of the public as we tried to walk, falling over each other and laughing. It were days like that, all precious memories.

Household Games

I can honestly say we had a happy life, but sometimes life was hard. There were times when money was an issue, like so many families we made ends meet. Money sometimes is not the "do all and end all" in life, although yes it does help. The children didn't really go short of anything and in the early years we lived on what we could afford from catalogues. It was especially hard when the time of year came to buy school uniforms. The pressure that children pass on to other children is hard, regarding who has the new up to date clothing trends. As parents we feel this pressure more than the children, but with Simon he honestly couldn't care less. He was so easy to buy for as he didn't go for trends or fashion. He was grateful for anything we bought him; even in his teenage years he didn't change he was a considerate, caring boy.

The household was happy, busy and loud. Family games came out most weekends, Scrabble with Simon was a joy, and how he found so many three and four letter words astounded me. Monopoly was too serious. All the children were bankrupt within half an hour of play, especially with Pete playing to the rule book, "I owe you" slips were not allowed. Simon and Natalie often played together contentedly as long as Natalie had total control. Simon went along with this to avoid the ear bashing from her.

They would go upstairs to rehearse a play, and then insisted that Pete and I sit for the performance of Hansel and Gretel. They would make do with sheets and bath towels for the costumes and any props they could use. We would sit and watch intently, stifling the need to laugh and applauding when necessary. They did however get up to mischief. Many a time, I found upon inspecting my expensive perfume and Peter's aftershave, which they had been mixing together to make their own potions. On the quite though, I found the aroma from these concoctions rather nice I didn't tell them this as they didn't need further encouragement.

In the winter, when the dark nights came in so early and the television got all too tedious, we made our own fun. It was a game Pete had made up and it frightened the life out of us all. He would turn all the lights off in the house and we would play "blood of a pig". We would be given only minutes to find a hiding place, and then Pete would come in search of us all. Natalie and I were too frightened to hide alone and we would go in search of a place where he hopefully wouldn't find us. We were petrified. Why we played I don't know as my heart used to race with fear. Simon and Stuart bravely went off alone, we would hear Pete growl "I want the blood of a pig" Nearer and nearer he would approach, reaching in the dark, feeling every nook and cranny. Simon always gave himself away by nervously giggling from his hiding place. Pete always found him first. "I want the blood of a pig" came the growling voice louder and louder, then the victim was trapped and Pete would have Simon.

He went for the neck mimicking that of a vampire, but because of Peter's whiskers on his unshaven chin it tickled and hurt at the same time and there was no escape. Pete was too strong but Simon would pounce given the chance and a wrestling match would begin. Lampshades, ornaments, anything near, thrown to one side in the pitch black rooms. Natalie and I would then take the chance to escape downstairs to safety while Pete was distracted by Simon, getting the blood of the pig. When normality resumed and the lights switched back on, the house resembled that of a passing tornado scene.

One of my favourite memories from their childhood was a particular Christmas. Simon was now nine years old and we always encouraged their belief in Santa. Childhood is such a small part of life; it should be treasured and held onto as long as possible. Growing up comes too soon, so when the children on many occasions, questioned the authenticity of Santa Claus, we were there to put any doubts of his being out of their heads. Deep down they really did want to believe, but some of the other children at school put a dampener on this belief. This was probably going to be the last Christmas that they truly believed in Santa, so we tried to make it special for them. Pete bought an inflatable Santa's outfit; we hatched a plan then waited for nightfall. After teatime, I sat the children in front of the television to watch the traditional festive movie, "Scrooge".

Pete went outside to the back garden; he placed ladders against the flat kitchen extension roof which was directly below Simon's bedroom window. I quickly helped him into his Santa suit, whilst watching for the children. I zipped him up, then with a Pritt stick in my hand, I dabbed his eyebrows and moustache area and stuck cotton wool to the sticky areas, so now he had eyebrows, moustache and beard. Then with the Santa hat in place, he was ready to impersonate the great man. The suit was deflated so I turned on the fan in the buttock area to inflate him but it was so noisy it sounded more like a light aircraft and I laughed so loud that it was a wonder the children didn't hear me. The scene was set to act out our plan, I told him to give me five minutes before he climbed the ladder to the roof, I went back in the sitting room and said to the children "listen" but no response came, again I said "listen" but they were all in full awe of the "Ghost of Christmas Past." At last they all looked up with puzzled expressions and I said "I am sure I can hear Santa's sleigh bells". Quietly they cocked their heads to one side and I muted the TV. "I can hear the bells, quick upstairs, we might just catch him" They jumped up together and climbed the stairs two at a time. At Simon's window, three little faces waited eagerly for signs of Santa and his reindeers, "shush" I told them. "Look" squealed Simon, then Pete, slowly and casually strolled past the window, waving gracefully, more like the Queen!

He had a black bin bag slung over his shoulder and I watched their expressions turn to shock then to delight. "Santa Santa" they excitably shouted to him, and then Pete gave a loud "Ho Ho Ho" before disappearing out of sight. The funny thing was, not one of the children noticed the loud whirring off the fan that trailed Pete. Simon said "where's dad, get dad", "oh no" I thought, this might get tricky. "He's downstairs, Iwill fetch him, don't you lot move, he might come back" then I was off as fast as I could. I met Pete at the back door, I ripped off his wool facial hair, which made his eyes water, then quickly helped him out of his suit, just as he walked into the kitchen the children were there to meet him.

" Dad, dad you missed him," they all said together, "No I didn't, I saw him, riding away on his sleigh" he said. I looked at Simon and noticed a little knowing smirk appear on his face but I think the fact that Pete had bits of cotton wool still stuck to his face in large clumps somehow gave the game away. It was years later, when the children were all in their teens, I talked to them about Santa on the roof, thinking that they knew all along it was dad, but to our shock and horror, they didn't have a clue, and they had thought it was the real Santa. I kicked myself for letting it slip, if I hadn't had told them it was dad, who knows, they might have always wondered whether Santa existed or not.

When the boys were small Pete had the use of a storage yard. He was self-employed and the yard was used for storage of Porta cabins and Containers. It was owned by a large building contractor and Pete worked many weekends restoring these cabins. The boys went with him on many occasions, giving me a well earned break from them and a chance to tidy the home. I made them all my famous pack up lunches as they would be gone for the day. The boys enjoyed going with dad, he didn't have to ask them twice, and they jumped at the chance. The yard was on an industrial estate, which was mainly closed at weekends, but had farm fields on one side so they could run about and enjoy themselves without bothering any of the locals. Here they ran wild and played "Cowboy and Indian" games whilst Pete got on with the job in hand. Often Pete would include the boys in his work but it wasn't easy to get Simon involved, no way was he going to do any work. Pete would find him sitting on a cabin roof, swinging his legs and refusing to come down. Looking back over these times, one could find it hard to imagine Simon doing manual work of any kind, especially if it required energy.

The times they got themselves into trouble were endless. Pete was in the middle of repairing a cabin and was stripping down an old unused one as he wanted to recycle parts of it to put to use on the newly repaired one, but on approaching the old cabin he found that the boys had already partially scrapped it, Doors, windows all gone to construct their den. Pete was furious that a seven and ten year old had managed to scrap and dismantle a cabin within an hour. Also there was the time when they invented a new game, not at all funny, certainly not to Pete. Simon had acquired a bit of old hose pipe and in one end of it he placed stones, then he chased Stuart around the yard flicking them at him.

That was bad enough, but then he turned his attention to Peter's van but after numerous shots at the windows he got bored and went onto something else. It was time to go and the boys were in the van waiting for dad. Pete jumped in and noticed that the side window was full of little holes, "who's done this" he angrily asked the boys, the little mucky faces looked up at him and innocently replied "not us dad." They did however actually learn a lot on these visits to the yard.

Highschool Days

The start of High School was drawing near. Simon would be just eleven when he was to start. He was still very young in his looks and his personality. He still carried his baby weight and was very small for his age with clear bright blue eyes and straight blonde hair, he was such a cutie. He still had a lisp which he had not grown out of, and never would. It made him dribble when he talked excitably, we used to laugh with him when he wiped his chin, then he would laugh at us and do it more to exaggerate the situation. He approached me once and lifted up his t-shirt and proudly showed me his two bellies and how he could make his two stomach tyres talk by squeezing them together. He had a thing about playing with his stomach, like drawing faces on it and proudly showing off to Natalie, who he now called "Tilly" but she wasn't impressed when he showed her what he could do.

It was one Saturday afternoon that I came very close to taking Simon to A &E. After taking a bath, he came downstairs to show me mysterious marks all over his stomach, face and neck I worried how these marks had just appeared as they weren't there that morning. I performed the "glass test", to check for meningitis and it didn't look good. I was now well into panic mode but he just sat completely calm and unflinching. I shouted to Pete that I was not happy and would he run us to the hospital, "wait a minute" Pete shouted from upstairs, as I put on my shoes and coat. Pete came into the room grinning like a Cheshire cat, "Simon" he said "what have you been playing with in the bath" Simon thought hard about this question and replied "nothing, why?" Pete held out his hand and showed me a soap dispenser that always sat on the bath. "Watch" he said to me and he pressed the applicator onto his skin and plunged down on it. With a pop, he released it and surprise surprise, the marks left behind were those similar to the ones on Simon's body.

"Oh" Simon said "I was playing with that". This is one of many incidents Simon panicked us with. Then there was the time he stuck the kitchen plunger onto his forehead and shuffled around imitating a Dalek, it was lucky for him we were not going out that day because the mark stayed on his head for a good hour afterwards.

With a couple of weeks before the start of term Simon decided he was now old enough to shave, which he did, although he had nothing to shave off yet. He was impatient to get started but Simon being Simon, he made a mess of that too and he came downstairs with half an eyebrow. Apparently he was trying to shape his eyebrows and got carried away. He came down smiling and feeling a bit foolish, he avoided my eyes so I wouldn't see, and when I eventually did, he raised his eyebrow and shrugged his shoulders. His eyebrow raising was a genetic gift, something he did when he was trying to be smooth and sophisticated. Luckily for him his eyebrow grew back quickly but nothing Simon did any more surprised us.

With the start of High School it meant the dreaded school uniform shopping trip. Shopping for Simon was frustrating as he had a chubby waist and short legs, so the pants we bought for him had to be altered, but he never complained and he would wear anything we bought him. Clothed in new pants, shirt, blazer and tie, along with the school badge on his pocket, he looked all grown up and very smart, ready for a new path in his life. Usually children are bought new school uniforms when they grow out of theirs but not Simon, we didn't get that far as his would be in tatters after only a few months. He had the habit of chewing through his collars and pushing his fingers through his cuffs, this was something he did well into his adult life. One thing let him down, his beautiful shoulder length hair, it was far too long and he needed it cutting but on suggestion of this, he wasn't happy, there was no way he would have this done. "I'm not bothered mum if it's too long, it's up to me how I have my hair" and he was right, but I was thinking of how the other children would react. After endless hours of persuasion we came to a deal, we would buy him a mobile phone if he had a haircut. I know it's bribery but it worked, it broke my heart watching his beautiful hair fall from his shoulders and in an instant he had the looks of a much older boy. Before he looked like a little "Dennis the Menace" but now he looked like an older one. The day came and I sat nervously waiting for Simon to come downstairs. He went to meet the school bus on his own knowing no one and within two months my little lad had suddenly grown up.

For the next six months Simon took everything in his stride, he didn't tell me much about the day to day goings on, but this was Simon. He told me things, happy things and what he had been taught in class, but stories he thought would upset me he kept to himself. I know some children taunted him about his lisp; it was others who told me, not Simon. He went through life like that; he didn't burden me with anything upsetting. Natalie and Stuart came home with all types of stories, but Simon didn't and I never questioned him. If he wanted to talk, he knew he could talk to me, Simon was secretive with his thoughts, and he always was.

Simon started keyboard lessons at school and he seemed to really enjoy it so we bought him a keyboard for Christmas. He was quite talented so we encouraged him in this venture, he couldn't read the music but he could listen to a piece and then play it on his keyboard. He would retreat to his bedroom for hours on end, perfecting his performance, we didn't mind the noise, and it was nice to hear he was happy and contented.

One Sunday afternoon he called to us to come upstairs, "I have written a song with music, you won't laugh will you" he said blushing, "we won't laugh" I promised. Eventually we persuaded him to play "I love you, I do, I love you, I really love you" and on and on he sang. It wasn't Mozart, but it was Simon doing something he truly believed in. "Simon that was fantastic you're a natural" we praised him and the buzz he got from that comment lifted him tremendously. It was so sweet, he tried so hard to please and he carried on this love for music for another twelve months or so.

Simon's pain tolerance was non- existent. He couldn't stand pain and the dreaded day came at school for the TB vaccinations, there was no avoiding it, he knew this and dreaded it months in advance. While waiting in line for his turn to arrive he was starting to turn pale and it didn't help that each child who came out of the surgery, made a point of informing poor Simon how the needle was as long as a pencil and just as thick and how the nurse came running at them from a head start. All this was too much for Simon and his colour turned to green. Without warning he fainted, he had always been the same, whenever he hurt himself, he would always turn ashen then announce "Oh, Oh I need a poo". Even when he had his tattoo done upon entry to the Army, he stopped the tattooist in mid flow, "Oh! I need a poo" he said much to the amusement of the shops occupants.

He tried hard at school and had a good relationship with his teachers. The parent's evenings were a delight to attend, I was so proud of him. However he wasn't so sweet and innocent as he led me to believe, he was a practical joker and he enjoyed making his school mates laugh. I think it was because he was so small, he had to try hard to fit in, and anything that made him stand out helped the cause. On one occasion at school, one of his teachers's had a framed photograph of her own children on her desk and Simon superimposed his face onto the photograph. He then asked her were they her children in the photograph and when she looked at it she noticed Simon's face amongst them. I wasn't told this at the time and only recently found out. Stories like this are only coming to me now, showing a side to Simon that I didn't know about.

We were open with our children and many Sunday nights, after tea, we would sit together in the lounge with no television or other distractions and talk together. It got heated sometimes but that was what it was all about, we talked about the dangers of drugs, alcohol and smoking. We talked a lot in those days and looking back I believe it made them into better adults. We thought we knew our children, but one day Simon gave us the shock of our lives, he did something that was totally out of character for him. We had only nipped out for an hour and ten minutes after we arrived back home, Simon came in and shouted he was tired and was going to bed. I looked at the clock, it was only seven pm. Pete and I exchanged glances, "I will check on him in a minute" I said, as it was unheard of for Simon to have an early night. I gave it ten minutes then I climbed the stairs to check on him, upon entering his room, I was shocked "Oh my God, Simon, what's wrong with you?" He was sat upright on his bed, legs crossed underneath him; his face was pale and clammy. Then the smell of alcohol hit me, he was drunk, and that was an understatement. He was completely legless and had vomited everywhere, I shouted Pete, we both stood shocked, and then he said something that I will never forget. He looked up at me with tears rolling down his face, "I am sorry mum, I have let you down". He said this over and over again, "I won't let you down again" he sobbed. Pete showered him while I made up a clean bed, he looked so sorry, and embarrassment was spread across his face, I could tell he was genuinely sorry for what he had done.

We put him to bed and constantly watched over him as he fell into a deep sleep. The next day, at one pm, I heard quiet tip toes sneaking down the stairs. He lingered for a minute outside the room where I was sitting and when he came in, head bowed, eyes to the floor, I said to him "you haven't let me down Simon, you have just learnt a lesson in life." He looked up and said "it's ok, I won't drink again". I didn't speak of it again with Pete as Simon was well aware of what he had done.

Simon had a good rapport with his teachers, below are two examples of their special memories of him.

<u>Mrs. J Porteous.- Head of Modern Languages.</u>
I taught Simon for 5 years for German, and my memory of him is a cheerful, good humoured young man with a cheeky smile who was eager to please and very popular with his peers. Simon was very enthusiastic in class and loved to speak German, even if he did struggle with the grammar! I remember that he found it difficult to learn his presentation for his speaking exam and decided to sing it to a familiar tune to help him memorize the words! Quite an unusual method! Simon was always interested in the little photos I kept of my children on my desk, which obviously changed over the years as they grew up. In year 11, Simon gave me a passport sized copy of his school photo (another pupil did the same) and asked me to put it on my desk so that he was part of the family!! I no longer have the photo on my desk but I have kept it in my box of special treasures. I will always have fond memories of dear Simon and I feel privileged to have known him.

<u>B. Fenney. Classroom Assistant.</u>
I was with Simon's class for both German and English. Among the students he was always known as "little Si"
I remember well an incident where, during a German class, Simon had covered up the faces of Mrs. Porteous children on the photograph on her desk with his own photo and then asked her if the picture were of her children!

I'm not sure in which classroom this incident occurred, I remember wandering around helping the students when I noticed Simon with one hand down his trousers and a small finger poking out of a hole near his trouser zip. I suggested that it was not really appropriate to be doing that during class. He asked if I thought it was another part of his anatomy poking through his trousers. I said "no" but I'm sure he believed it was something other than a finger! Needless to say, with the students comprising mostly boys, it was not long before everyone in the class was made aware of the hole in Simon's trousers.

When the end of Simon's school years came, he was proud of what he had achieved, although his exam results were not of a genius, he did the best he could. He had to put together a record of achievement for the preparation for work, that one day he was to find.

9/11

Simon was just fourteen when the murderous events of 9/11 happened in America. I remember clearly we all sat together watching these events unravel on the TV. Despite 9/11 having a huge effect to the whole of the world, I never thought for a second that it 9/11 would become the first stage of what would be Simon's fate. The children sat and watched, but not with much understanding, how could we have known that Simon would die because of the consequences of that day when he was merely fourteen years old. He was a child, playing like other children, having no concept of the threat that now looms over us, how war escalates. Within seven years, Simon would grow and mature, and join the front line to fight a war that started when he was just a boy. If 9/11 hadn't come to destroy the piece, there was a slight chance that the lads would not even be in Afghanistan today; Simon would still be walking amongst us. Simon's fate was set in stone the day 9/11 began.

Butterflies and Feathers

Highschool days

Friends

Simon's school was a fine one; it was situated in Culcheth, not in our home town. Because of this he didn't have friends at home so when he took an interest in rugby I was pleased, it would give him the opportunity to meet people who were local and of the same age. He was still very small for his age, still carried his chubby puppy fat, very cute and very cheeky. It was at the Rhino's Rugby Club, which was situated in Cadishead that Simon met his true friend Mattie. The players at the club, who were mostly big strong lads and towered above Simon, took him under their wing, but despite this he would still aggravate them constantly. They were rough with him, but all in good humour. Dave Butler (Butler), who was one of the players, is well over six foot tall and always bore the brunt of Simon's aggravation. Simon would dig at him and Butler would give chase but Simon being small and nippy, would always outrun him. When Simon least expected it, Butler would come behind him, hold him in a head lock and rub his head hard. This is what it was like, over and over again but Simon never refused to give up and always had the last laugh.

Simon and Mattie were like chalk and cheese in appearance, Mattie is a big lad, Simon so small, but their personalities were identical. Mattie's appearance is that of a much older lad for his age, they grew close whilst training together. Simon didn't't take rugby seriously while Mattie did and he still plays for the Rhino's today. In training Simon would take the ball and run towards the "Try Line" with Mattie in hot pursuit but Simon would giggle when he saw he was being chased and would collapse with laughter as Mattie descended on him, bringing him down with a hard tackle. Then a wrestling match would start between the two of them as the other players looked on with arms crossed, cursing this childish behaviour, their coach, Steve, would be fuming at them.

Simon sometimes got the job of lines man for the Rhino's, when they had a home game but this was a bad idea as Simon was biased. I attended many matches when Simon held the flag and on occasions when he stood under the sticks, as the Rhino's kicked for goal, he lifted the flag when it hadn't even been a goal this was much to the opposition's shout of cheats and angry looks. It didn't bother Simon; he walked back to the line with a cheeky smirk on his face. I would say to him "Simon you can't do that" "It was in, mum" he would reply, lifting his eyebrow and winking at me.

The appreciation for Simon came when the Rhino's had a presentation night for the children's team and Simon was awarded the "Club Trophy" for all he contributed to the club. He was as proud as punch with this trophy and now he knew he belonged to something, part of something he had always longed for. He was never going to be a great rugby player, he knew that and so did we but he was happy at just attending.

Mattie and Simon's friendship became a special one that would last for years, only to be broken with Simon's death. He told Mattie everything, things he couldn't tell his family that was the way my son was. There were two sides to Simon, the way we saw him and a different side when he was with others outside the family. We were only told the things that Simon wanted us to hear. He didn't brag to us or complain, he didn't tell us his worries or his concerns, he was just our Simon. Others however saw a different, more mature side to him.

Towards the end of his school life he started to alter. He had grown leggy and lanky, his feet appeared far too large for him but he still held on to his cuteness, with that slight lisp of his, which sometimes made him dribble a bit when he talked excitedly. Simon was full of life; he left an impression on every person he met, his sarcastic humour and his laid back manor always in the forefront. If he could amuse people, he would be happy. We could be walking along the street where the public were busily going about their business and when he came to a lamppost, he would casually walk up to it and would look the other way, as if he hadn't noticed the post. Then as he drew closer he would kick it, making a noise, as his head made near contact with the post. He pretended he had walked into it, and then he would fall about rubbing his head, appearing in pain as the public looked on, concerned at this poor boy that had just walked into a lamp post and hurt his self. This made us look terrible because we were laughing at this unfortunate lad.

Ann Annis

I don't know what Simon's outlook on life was because it was something we didn't ask our teenagers. All I do know is that he tried his best to enjoy every waking day, very rarely did I see him down and fed up, and even in sad times, he always managed a smile.

Simons career decisions

The exams were looming, Simon found them difficult, he was a hand on type of person like his dad. Classroom was a boring issue with Simon, he didn't do too well, although he tried, he just wasn't that way academically. He would have loved a career with animals but he had no qualifications to pursue this so he didn't have a clue what he was to do. While he was thinking about his next move, he went to work with his dad as a construction worker. He looked so comical, so small; I named him "Bob the Builder." His hard hat was huge, it covered his face down to his nose and it wobbled with every head movement. His steel toecap boots were heavier than him and the crutch of his work pants dangled down to his knees but he got on with it and saved most of his wages up.

An opportunity came up, an apprenticeship with a large well known house builder; he would train as a joiner which meant college one day a week. I know this wasn't what Simon had intended to do but there wasn't much going at the time, so he gave it a go. It was a start, a foot on the ladder, my dedicated son plodded and persevered with this job, his place of work was far from home, so at five am each morning he would set off on his bicycle, with his heavy rucksack of tools and his much needed pack up lunch.

He wouldn't arrive home until six thirty or later, he was a trier, his determination was a credit to him. It wasn't a breeze for him at work either, he worked with full time laborers and they took advantage of him, "do this, get that" etc., which he did without question. Roger and Stumpy were two of the workers and they took Simon under their wing and taught him as well as they could, the ways of joinery. He worked well with these two, although he was slow to pick up the trade, they persevered with him .He hated college which was situated in the rougher part of the city, these surroundings were different to what he was used to. Simon rarely ventured far from his home town of Cadishead, which is a small and friendly place where everybody knows each other, so college opened his eyes to a different way of life and to people who were scary to him.

Some of them were very rough in the way they spoke or acted. Simon said they didn't learn much and that it was just a place to hang out for them, they didn't take college seriously. Looking back at those times, this career did not suit Simon; he was meant for a better, more challenging job.

He had some good times at work, with Roger and Stumpy, they were good role models and taught Simon well. He left memories with everybody who knew him. At work one day he was stoking up the fire in the yard, I could have warned them that Simon had a fascination with fire and a small controlled blaze could turn into a bonfire in Simon's presence. The fire was to get rid of all the rubbish that lay around the yard and Simon stood guard over it, making sure it didn't go out, only this time the flames got the better of him when he poured petrol over it. It went "whoosh", the flames went high into the air, it leapt at Simon and set his pants on fire. He then ran round the yard patting down his legs and stripped off his clothes in front of the workers. Roger and Stumpy laughed, luckily he was ok, and he came home that night stinking of smoke and his clothes in tatters.

One day at work he was told he was to be sent to a Liverpool site but there was no way he could get there as it was too far away, especially on his bicycle. But that was not for a while yet and he had started driving lessons. We helped to pay for the lessons but he did save some money to put towards them. They were costly and we didn't mind giving him a helping hand. It took him four attempts to pass his test, the three fails were depressing for him but he needed a car and eventually passed. Now the hard work began to find him a suitable cheap vehicle. He couldn't afford much but with our contribution he purchased a small older Ford Fiesta. I worried each and every time he got behind the wheel but I expect that all mothers do. This car was a godsend, the travel to work was far better than that on a bicycle. But being Simon, all good things come to an end, when just weeks later the engine blew up and Pete had to tow back his wrecked car from the motorway. He only had "Third Party Insurance " so no claim was made, poor Simon was devastated, nothing went smoothly for him, so back on his bike he got. It played on our minds, we felt sorry for the lad and a week later whilst passing a garage,

Pete and I spotted a very cheap old Citroën. Not a car one would normally see an 18 year old boy driving but when we brought it home for him he was so grateful, he didn't care what it looked like, it was a car and that's all that mattered. So with the promise of "I will pay you back mother", he put in his radio cd player and the largest Boom Box he could afford, went in the boot. There wasn't any room for anything else as it was gigantic and his favourite "Eminem" songs bounced off the car windows. It was comical to see a much older person's car with a young driver behind the wheel and a large Boom Box sticking out of the small boot. We still have that Boom Box in our loft and since we have put a new loft cover on, we can't get it out!

Life flowed on for Simon, training as a joiner wasn't easy for him, but he was advancing and actually looked like he would eventually have a career in this field of work. However one night Simon came home from work and I immediately knew from the look in his eyes that something wasn't right. He was devastated, all the tools he took so long to collect, so much money spent, had all been stolen whilst in storage overnight. He had one solitary hammer left, he didn't have the money to replace these items, yet he needed these vital tools to do his job so that night Pete and Simon sat in front of the computer and brought up a Tool Station Shop on line.

He wouldn't pick anything, he felt terrible having to rely on mum and dad again, he truly didn't want us to buy him the items he needed and would have gone without. It took a long time to pick replacement tools out for him, screwdrivers, drill and drill bits and a saw, in fact everything he needed. All the time, as he reluctantly pointed out what he needed, he repeated "are you sure, I feel awful for this?" I smiled and said to him "when you are rich and famous you can look after us." After a lengthy spell he had all he needed. He had achieved his NVQ's and it looked certain that this is what he would be doing for the foreseeable future.

As time went on we could see Simon becoming more and more withdrawn and increasingly disinterested in his work, it wasn't that he was lazy, it was just something that he didn't want to do. He had given it a go, it was beginning to depress him, and this wasn't healthy for a lad so young. Pete sat him down one day and said to him that nothing in this life was worth the amount of upset this job was burdening him with and he must look for an alternative career. Simon left his job, "so what now?" he didn't know, he had no money so he started helping Pete out again, just for a little while, just for pocket money. He worked hard whilst with Pete, he had the same laid back manner as his dad, and they all got along great and had a good working relationship.

They had their moments at work, good and bad and tried to make working life humorous as well. One particular day whilst Pete, Simon and another work colleague were standing chatting, Simon's close connection with animals surfaced again when a large grey squirrel came from nowhere and raced up his leg, Shocked, they all stared and waited for Simon's reaction but it didn't come, there wasn't one and he just looked down as though this was normal behaviour for a squirrel.

It was really hard graft, especially in the winter months, they both arrived home each night mudded up wet and cold, I made them strip in the porch and then they would race to see who got a bath first. Simon kept his thoughts mainly to himself, he would think about things and only release his thoughts when he was good and ready. One particular day he felt that he needed to share his thoughts with us and out of the blue announced "I'm thinking of joining the Army". I sat in shock, "where had this come from?" and thinking back over the years, the Army was the last thing I thought Simon would be interested in. "Simon a Soldier?", no this wasn't him, I didn't know what to think but eventually I thought why not, there was absolutely nothing out there that was remotely suited to Simon. Even if he had continued with his apprenticeship there was no certainty that he would have been offered a permanent job. I suggested college as he wanted to work with animals and why not study for this, but we all knew it was far out of his reach, just a pipe dream.

We sat and talked about the pros and cons of this idea, Simon seemed very positive about his decision. I said to him "you will need to put in 100% commitment, its hard work". Back then the Afghan conflict was still in the background on the news and to tell you the truth I didn't know much about what was going on there. If I had, I don't know what I would have said to him but I do know one thing that Simon listened to us and valued our advice and if I had shown my upset at the idea of him joining the Army he wouldn't have gone through with it.

We have to let our children make their own decisions in life and unfortunately this is one that I will regret for the rest of my life. I didn't know how serious Simon was on this idea of his but I found out a few days later, after he had been to the Army Careers Office in Manchester for advice. Pete took him and waited anxiously, the ball was rolling, he had taken his first step, he had an initial interview, he was then was booked in for written and medical tests. It was a long process and it gave me relief to know that he could change his mind if he wished to.

In such a short time my little man grew taller, lean and strong, his legs resembled lengths of string with massive flipper feet but still he maintained his cute young looks, he still had his sense of humor and was always comical, so laid back and totally hilarious at times with his off the cuff remarks. He was a good natured lad with a heart of gold who would genuinely do anything for anybody. In the meantime Simon carried on working with Pete whilst waiting for an enrolment date to join the Army.

Ann Annis

Simon short joinery career

Simon's home life

Natalie met her boyfriend Nick just before her 16th birthday in March 2006; they chatted on the internet and set a day to meet one another. Much to Natalie's annoyance, Simon intervened and told her he would drive her to meet Nick. He loved his sister and they had a very special bond and now he was getting older he felt it was his role to care and watch over her. He grew protective of her and with Natalie in his car they picked up Nick. He was unnerved by the presence of Simon who had a wide grin fixed on his face the whole of the car journey. Simon enjoyed aggravating Nick and with him being a quiet type, he didn't know how to take him and his sarcastic ways. Natalie is quite bad tempered and I remember her ticking Simon off on many occasions for aggravating Nick, but he found all this humorous and I'm sure he did it all the more just to annoy his sister. As time went on, he and Nick grew close and Simon accepted this lad into our family.

Simon's presence in the home was that of joy but very unpredictable, he was always up to something. It was either Simon hurting himself due to his clumsiness or him trying to tell a joke that he messed up every time, there were no boring moments. The home was lively and sometimes in chaos and it all came from Simon. The poor dog would be sent crackers as he wouldn't leave him alone and constantly tormented him and it would take hours to get him to settle down after being wound up. He treated Mojo like he was his "Lion King", always lifting him head high whilst shouting "Simba".

Mojo did however get his own back on his faithful master. One afternoon, after a large Sunday lunch, we all retired to the lounge and put the TV on to watch a good old matinee, and normally when we did this we napped all the way through it. Simon always lay on the floor, head propped up, Mojo always lay snuggled up against him. All was quiet when Simon suddenly jumped up, wafting his hand in front of his face "Mojo, you dirty dog" he shouted and I gathered that Mojo had made a nasty pong and Simon wasn't amused. All went quiet again; the dog was soundly asleep next to Simon. I wondered what Simon was doing when he quietly, stealthily, got to his feet and crept, without a sound over to Mojo. He lowered his backside onto Mojo's back without waking him, then he trumped on the dog' back in revenge for his earlier gift. .The dog shot up looked around disgruntled then disappeared quickly to the kitchen into his bed where he stayed for the next hour. I cried laughing; this was just one of those spontaneous moments with Simon.

Whilst in the process of Army recruitment, Simon endeavored to reach full fitness. He would go out weighted down with a rucksack, inside it was a one litre plastic bottle filled with water and he would run for miles. He and Mattie would then go to the gym or for a few rugby training sessions in between. He would come home all hot and sweaty and flex his muscles like "Mr. Universe" or offer Pete a challenge to an arm wrestle, giggling and collapsing on the floor when Pete got the better of him. He couldn't take anything seriously and I remember he came back once after a long and tedious run and was rubbing his chest. I asked him what was wrong; he laughed, lifted his t-shirt and showed me his shaven nipple which was annoying him now. "What have you done that for, stupid boy?" I said, as he shrugged his shoulders and told me he wanted a nice smooth belly. This wasn't the first time he decided to shave off his body hair. Simon was really toning up with all his hard work although he still had his flabby boobies, which sometimes bore the brunt of our jokes with him.

His favorite musician was "Eminem." He had a fine collection of his music and constantly played his music. I would be talking to Simon when he would start to sing, with arms going and legs kicking to the beat, he would raise those hilarious eyebrows whilst bellowing out the tunes. He would sing hopelessly out of tune but personally I think he did this purposely. Throughout his career I have heard stories of how Simon would burst out singing at the drop of a hat and totally unexpectedly. He had a clever way of making a sound like a Boom Box with his mouth, making his own music. I have seen this done on the TV but haven't a clue what it is called but Simon did this well. Even when I was feeling down he would do this rap and I was soon cheered up. Simon was obsessed with Eminem, he knew the star fought hard for his celebrity status and had achieved stardom through some really hard times, so his music meant a lot to Simon, it told a story and he admired him immensely.

Simon didn't have a serious side, even when I needed him to listen to me. I tried to tell him constantly to "sit down for a pee" and I would shout this from the bathroom on numerous occasions, when I stood with feet drenched from Simon's last visit to the toilet. "It's bloody everywhere" I would shout and he would find it this amusing, Pete used to nickname him "Swampy "on these occasions.

Simon and Mattie spent a lot of time together before his entrance into the Army. I didn't know what they actually got up to but I assumed they were doing what all lads at that age do, hanging about in each other's homes, playing football and it's only when our boy had sadly left us that I found out a few little tales of the mischief they got up together. Here are tales told by Mattie:-.

When Dobber was 18 years old, we met at the Trafford Centre one time, we were bored and didn't have anything to do, so we went for races in our cars around Trafford Park, we found a street about a quarter mile long and would have drag races down this long street, emptying our boots to make it fair.

When we were both 18 years, we used to go to the Coach and Horses pub, we would meet at mine, Dobber would make us get a can of beer from the off license, then tell the man in the shop he was under age, just to aggravate.

When Dob was home for Xmas 2008, he was at my house, he didn't bother knocking, he just came in, we would go out at 12pm for an all-day session, then back to mine for a shower and to get dressed, I once got out of the shower and he was stood at the top of the stairs, with the front door open, the curtains open, and he was lifting weights completely naked.

One time over Christmas 2008, Simon and me were in Irlam having a drink, at last orders we went over the road to the Chinese chip shop, we gave our orders and the lady went out the back to get them, I dared Simon to take their clock, so he, without hesitation climbed over the counter and took the round clock off the wall, he hid it under his t-shirt, and I could see the outline of it, when the lady came out Simon asked her for the time, she looked round to the clock, she looked confused then she looked at Simon and he gave it her back laughing, she gave us our food then barred us from coming in again.

Two weeks before Simon was to leave, we went to the pub, I tried to get Simon drunk so he would open up and talk to me, I needed to know if there was any requests if he didn't make it home, Simon wouldn't talk about this, but he did say, look after Tilly for me, and Mattie out of all my mates from the Army and outside you are the best, I love you.

There are more stories but I think it's best if I stick to the tame ones. Simon and Mattie were more like brothers than best mates, they were great together and I thank Mattie for being a true loyal friend to my son. If I had known what the pair got up to there would have been harsh words and that's why I was never told before.

Mummies little soldier

On the 12th August 2006, at the age of 19 years, Simon went off to join the physically demanding Infantry Training Course at ITC Catterick, where he joined the Queen's Division, 8 Platoon. On the day of his departure I knew I was to lose my son to adulthood, he was to go and spread his wings, to pursue the career he was proud to have chosen. While he readied himself, the lump in my throat hurt so much but I showed no sadness towards him, I didn't want him knowing that all of this was breaking my heart so we laughed and talked about what was to come. Our eldest son, Stuart, had done all this years ago when he joined the Royal Marines. I didn't know why but this was different. Dobber, my little one was going to start his life as an adult without me to guide him. He was ready but nervous and jittery not knowing what was in store for him as he packed his rucksack making sure he had everything on the list that the Army had given to him. This house was to be so quiet now! He would have to endure hard times in his quest to become a Soldier in the Army, never in this world would I have thought he would have chosen this career, to me he wasn't the Soldier type but one day he would prove me so wrong. Pete was to drive him to the railway station and he told me "I will ring, mother, as soon as I get the chance" and with a nervous sweet smile he was gone. From that day our lives were never the same and it was only then that I cried for my son.

Pete returned an hour or so later, he told me other lads were awaiting the same train as Simon, he said that he looked so young even amongst the other new recruits. An hour into the train journey Simon rung my mobile phone, thanking me for the pack up I gave him. Laughing he said "there's enough to feed an Army here mum", he was embarrassed by the size of it so he hid it from the others in his rucksack. I must admit I did go overboard with his pack up but I did with all the pack ups I have ever made, especially when the children were little and they went on school trips. I couldn't bear the thought of them not having enough to eat and everything went in, sandwiches, cakes, biscuits, crisps, chocolate and fruit. I think my children dreaded opening them in front of the others." I am a mum and I care", I used to tell them. After a long, anticipated journey, the new recruits were shown their dormitories, which were very basic and I suppose daunting for the new lads, but they would soon grow accustomed to their new environment and then the harsh training routine was to follow.

Simon managed to ring home often, he was buzzing at the prospect of the new activities being taught and the experiences of a completely new way of life, although it wasn't all happy times. He told me stories that upset me and played on my mind and all I wanted to do was to go and fetch him and bring him home. At one point I wanted to ring his Commanding Officer and give him a piece of my mind but this wouldn't have gone down well with Simon. At times he rang and told me he couldn't do it anymore, he'd had enough, but we would talk for a long time and afterwards he felt better. I think he just needed reassurance, he knew it wouldn't be easy and he had to be reminded of that. When he came home on weekends he didn't talk much about the goings on in camp and I knew it was Mattie he spoke to more.

The true professionalism in Simon was beginning to surface, he wouldn't talk work at home as work was work and it stayed there, also I knew he didn't want me to worry, he never did. We have a good family friend, John Royle, who was in the forces himself, a Sergeant with the Parachute Regiment and at times he helped Simon by talking to him and giving him advice and guidance and this helped him immensely. Simon often took things that were said to heart and thought he was being singled out and given punishment that he felt wasn't justly deserved so talking to John made better sense of the situation. Even on leave he strived to achieve maximum fitness, knowing this would help upon his return to camp, where the physically demanding fitness regimes started. He put 100% into his training and slowly but surely he began to understand what was to be expected of him. It was in Simon's early training days that the other lads at camp began to see him as the larger than life character he was at home. Being clumsy, a joker and a good friend, he was a genuine gentle lad who, when spirits were low, had a special way of lifting them, either by his sudden outburst of song and rap or by talk.

We received a letter one morning inviting us to a family day at Simon's camp so we could see all that he had achieved and learnt. Here we could see how he was living and the area he now called home. When we arrived at this large camp, I was quite surprised as it didn't look too bad. I had images of a "Colditz" style barracks but it wasn't, it was a nice large place in a beautiful part of Catterick. We could see that all the other parents had now been reunited with their sons but Simon was nowhere in sight and after an anxious wait ,we were told that Simon and the rest of his troop had been held back to go over a routine they had repeatedly messed up. I then spotted him, marching in step alongside his colleagues; I must have produced the largest, proudest grin because when he saw us, a little smile came from him. That day we were shown the many things he had been taught, machinery, ration packs etc. But it was all too much to take in. Simon was amongst a group showing families how to prepare the ration food over a little Calor gas stove, I watched intently and I knew Simon was avoiding my glare. He was trying to be serious today and if he looked, he would flash that cute smile and laugh. I could see the pride in him, it shone so bright, I could see how close Simon had become to his colleagues and the joy I received from the sight of seeing my son happy made it all worthwhile.

It had been a long and eventful day and we were to be treated to one more final march, to finalize the day. As I looked on at Simon's troop I could tell by the mischievous glint in Simon's eyes that he was contemplating something. I put my hands in front of my mouth to hide my laughter as he marched the wrong way, away from the lads at the front and as a result all the lads that were behind Simon followed him. I could see Simon's C.O. fuming with anger but Simon grinned like a Cheshire cat and I do believe he did that on purpose. Later he received the full pelt of anger from his C/O. While there, we got told of another little trick that Simon used to enjoy doing. When all the lads were out on parade and standing to attention on the parade ground, he would jab the lad next to him in his privates and as this lad looked at Simon, he looked the other way as if he hadn't a clue what had gone on. The lad then looked to his other side and jabbed the innocent lad in his groin area, so in turn this went right down the line, much to Simon's delight and amusement.

Simon's one hate was that of the gas tank, which they all had to train in. With gas masks in hand they would enter this tank and gas would be pumped into it. Only when instructed to do so do they put on their masks. It was a horrific part of training but vital, so that they were prepared in case they came across this fowl smelling lethal gas, whilst in combat. Simon found this area extremely difficult but eventually he passed, by sheer determination. He was doing very well, the difference in our son was remarkable, he had matured and still lacked some confidence but he wasn't as bad as he once was. Simon came home with us that weekend and I could tell he was pleased with what he had achieved over the past three months; he walked with his head held high. If Pete and I are walking around town, we can spot a soldier immediately out of the crowd, he has a walk only a soldier has; he has a manner only a soldier has; now our caring son had all these attributes and more.

Simon came home for Christmas 2006, he made the most of his time at home, and he knew that on his return, training was to be the toughest yet. He had the passing out parade in February, so on top of this, he had to prepare to reach his final milestone as he could easily get "back trooped" if he wasn't up to scratch and this is the last thing Simon would want as he had worked too hard and he wouldn't allow it to happen to him. He lapsed on his fitness over Christmas, the festivities got the better of him, too much food and far too much beer and he spent a lot of time out with Mattie. I didn't nag him or remind him to do his fitness training; he had earned this short spell of rest.

Like some Annis family members, Simon couldn't drink too much, he certainly tried to, but beer didn't like him and now as a trainee "Squaddie" he had picked up some bad habits, over excess of alcohol being one of them. He would fall through the door and try to climb the stairs as quietly as he could, but he was clumsy even when sober and when he was drunk he was far worse. Every wall, door or cupboard was an obstacle for him to battle with but the moment he fell into bed, the loud snoring would commence, then the sleep walking would start. Only when Simon was drunk did he do this and we would hear him in the kitchen looking for food. In the morning he wouldn't remember a thing. I always got up first the next morning to check where Simon was, before Natalie got up because after a heavy drinking session, for some unknown reason he awoke missing his boxer shorts.

The proudest day of my life

After many months of hard work we were preparing to attend Simon's passing out parade. He had done it; he had finally achieved his goal. It was February 9th 2007, we arrived at Catterick where so many proud parents stood waiting for the ceremony to begin, and it was to be a busy day with so much on the agenda. It was absolutely freezing cold, my feet were already numb and my hands were blue, we all made our way over to the parade ground where we were seated in readiness for what was to come, In the distance we heard the sounds of the glorious band approaching, the drums prominent then the battalion In perfect formation they approached, all pristine in their blues, white gloves, shining belts and berets with red and white hackles which proudly adorned their heads, It was perfect and immaculate, they proudly marched with expertise and control, heads held high and chins up. Then we spotted our Simon, he was camouflaged amongst his true comrades, my son, now a Royal Fusilier. He had completed his physical and demanding training and now he was ready to embrace the varied lifestyles on offer with the Royal Regiment of Fusiliers. As the parade passed by, they saluted the audience; I was in awe, not taking my tearful eyes off my son. He had achieved so much and I could see the pride and commitment in his eyes as he looked for his family in the busy crowd.

After the parade, we were to be entertained with a play that the lads were putting on for us. This time it was held in the warmth of the theatre and as we sat waiting for the performance to begin, we could hear the banter from the lads behind the curtain. We could see their silhouettes, they were running around trying to get into costume, we could hear their laughter they pushed each other over, they were now relaxed and enjoying themselves after the hard work they had endured over the past seven months. It was a very enjoyable show, a comedy, and when I saw Simon up there, it reminded me of when he was in his infant school play, dressed as a yellow bird with the beak covering his small face, as he danced to the"Birdie Song".

After the show, we met the new proud Fusiliers in the mess, where much appreciated hot drinks and food were laid out. Simon approached us, we hugged him, and he knew we were the proudest parents a son could have. Today he was to be told where he was going to be stationed, he hoped it would be Cyprus and as I watched him chatting and laughing amongst his friends, I knew that this was what he was destined to do, he was now part of the military family, and he would spend the majority of his life with them. Only on leave would he be part of our Annis clan.

For twenty years Simon and I were so close and now the natural rift would appear, it choked me to think that, but we fully supported him, this was his life now and I had to let go. We felt that we had done our job well by bringing up Simon to be the man he was. Simon approached us as we waited outside, excitement showed on his face, he was to be stationed in Cyprus, and he was delighted. We left him with Mattie, they were to follow us home within the hour but my feet were sore and I was tired and very cold, so we set off on our journey home.

He was home now, a full time professional soldier, all the training and hard work had paid off. The instant he walked through the door with hold all in hand, the house was totally unrecognizable, he had a presence that followed him, a very messy one. He didn't have a long break but he kept his fitness up and in between, saw Mattie. He enjoyed nights out, he was a more relaxed character now and had grown and matured more, he was now a man, not my little lad anymore. This was to be another busy year and he was apprehensive as Cyprus was a long way from home and most of his newly acquired friends were being posted elsewhere, so once again Simon was starting out in an unfamiliar place with unfamiliar people.

Simon went back to his barracks in Hounslow while awaiting his posting to Cyprus, it was around this time that he took up an interest in Poker and although I don't really agree with gambling, he had quite a flare for it. He announced that one day, when he retired, this would be his full time profession, he used to play on line on his lap top and he did actually win more than he lost, well that's what he told me. He didn't gamble large amounts of money, he was adamant this would be his future one day, he was lucky with money. Whilst in Hounslow, Simon's friend asked him if he would run him to the airport, naturally Simon said he would, so just in shorts and t-shirt he drove his friends to the airport.

After he had dropped them off he noticed he didn't have a drop of petrol for his return, he had no phone and no money with him so he sat pondering for a while then started ransacking the car for loose change. He managed to find £3, he had enough fuel left to get him to the local services, where you would think the £3 could be spent on petrol, but no, Simon walked into the services and popped it into the slot machines and he dropped £40. If he hadn't have won, he would have been walking back to the barracks. He filled the car with petrol, bought sweets and went on his way. If it had been anyone else they wouldn't have done this, they would have put £3 worth of petrol in the tank. That was Simon all over, act first, think later. This time it paid off for him.

Ann Annis

Simon standing proud

Overseas

Simon went to Cyprus a few short weeks after his Passing Out ceremony. The barracks were large and Simon had a balcony overlooking the beach, a sea front location with beautiful clear blue sea. There was a beach bar to chill out in, it sounded like an ideal holiday location but the bare brick buildings gave it away. It was anything but a holiday hotel. Simon found it hard to fit in here; a lot of the lads were older with more experience and had already completed their tours in Afghanistan or Iraq. He felt out of place and in one phone call home, he told me that until he had experienced life on the front line he couldn't give himself the credit of calling himself a soldier for real. No matter what I told him, it didn't alter his feelings, as far has he was concerned, he wasn't a fully-fledged Soldier until he had taken up arms against the enemy. He didn't like it here, but it was part of his tour and he would endure it and see it through. He did make some friends, mainly new young soldiers like himself, he drank a lot more here, the weather was hot and the bar easily accessible.

He rang as often as he could but I worried one time as we hadn't heard from him in a while, so when he eventually did ring, I was relieved. He explained that he didn't have a phone and that was because he had dropped it intentionally, from his balcony, not once but twice as he was bored and wanted to see how indestructible it was. After the first drop it still worked but after the second drop the phone was incapable of making any more calls so he bought another from the market. He rang and told me the phone he had now was fantastic, with all the latest gadgetry but shortly afterwards, this phone broke as well. When I come to think of it, anything electrical or motorized didn't last long in Simon's presence. He had managed to wreck two cars, endless numbers of mobile phones, two computers and that's just what I know of. I once found a handbook in his bedroom, entitled "Hacking for Beginners" His computer was missing one side panel off the hard drive and upon further inspection, tin foil had been placed inside to attach loose and alien wiring together. Consequently that computer didn't last long.

He was always losing things like watches and jewellery but he called these things, "just objects" and there was no point in losing sleep over such mundane items. When Simon was bored he would pick anything at hand to bits. I have a coffee table in the lounge, and underneath there were two ornamental metal balls but one is missing. I have looked everywhere for this ball but it has disappeared. The number of times, as a youngster, he would pick the plaster off his bedroom wall until the bare brick was exposed. I told him he was a walking wreaking machine, unintentionally or intentionally but I loved this little fidgeter and I wouldn't have changed him for the world. He persevered in Cyprus and often went drinking in the nearby town where little bars frequented the area. As mentioned earlier Simon wasn't a drinker, well he was, but his body wasn't. I have heard tales of how he would try to make his way back to camp, at the end of the night, but never arrived. The furthest he got to was the beach, where he lay down to sleep and it's only when the MPs (Military Police) found him, was he escorted back to the barracks. On the occasions that the MPs failed to find him, he would wake up, starry eyed, amongst the sunbathers, wondering how he had got there.

It was while he was still on tour in Cyprus that he was deployed to Jordan on a tough six week intensive training exercise. He didn't ring home during this time but he managed to get a message to me on the computer. They had leave due and took it while they were there. He said the place was amazing and an eye opener for him. He sent me pictures of the hotel and in his words, it was a Palace with marble archways and art covered lobbies. They were treated like royalty and although it was very draining and educational, the sights he took in were the things he could only have imagined. Whilst on leave they visited the good old USA. It was on this short leave that Simon encountered another side to life. On the inside he was a softie and was easily touched by the downfall of others. One time, he and his friends started a conversation with a down and out, a tramp they met on the side walk near their hotel after they had been for a stroll. Simon felt disgusted by how this pathetic looking man had to live so he invited him up to the hotel room where he was offered a shower and food. They gave him clothes and listened to him as he told them how he had succumbed to this life of misery. He said that a long time ago he had lost his family and everything he owned in life, due to the horrific wild fires. He had nothing, no insurance; nothing and he had now come to accept this way of life as every time he tried to establish himself it had failed miserably. He stayed in the company of Simon and his friends for a while, enjoying their hospitality and before he left, they gave him money but it wasn't long before he resumed his place on the pavement. After this meeting with the unknown tramp, Simon said to me "we don't realize how lucky we are." I know this broke Simon's heart, to see this lonely man go on his way. He didn't show these emotions to his friends, he kept them to himself.

Simon's Regiment was due back in Hounslow late 2007 but he was left behind after a terrible incident, I will outline what happened but I won't go into too much detail because I truly believe that what happened didn't get investigated to the extent it should have. Whilst in a bar in Cyprus with his friends, there was a scuffle, a bit of rowdiness amongst the lads, they had all had a little too much to drink and one lad in particular was the worse for wear. It resulted in Simon having a glass allegedly pushed into his face, which resulted in a large blood loss and him passing out. Although this incident went to Court internally, the lad was let off. The defense said that Simon had fallen onto the glass, but the scar on his face was a perfect crescent shape and I find it hard to believe that if he had fallen, wouldn't his natural instinct tell him to put his hand or arm out to protect his face. He wouldn't fall in a straight line with his arms down by his sides. Simon felt very let down when those mates who were with him refused to stand as witnesses. I find all of this very curious and I suppose I will never get to hear the truth. Simon stayed in the Cypriot hospital over Christmas as his wound was a terrible mess and he needed an operation to repair the large deep gash on his cheekbone. How could this happen? Are they not supposed to be brothers in arms? I was devastated which was made worse by the time of year.

The phone calls he made from his hospital bed upset me as he sounded in so much pain and so lonely. He didn't get over this incident and was always aware of the deep scar that the wound had left behind. After a week in hospital he received permission to leave for the UK. He had told me how bad it looked and I told him "it can't be that bad, I will tell you how it looks when I see you." I dreaded seeing him; I prepared myself and knew that I had to remain expressionless when I saw him, even if it was a dreadful sight.

He arrived back in the UK early 2008 and I waited anxiously for his return home, he had rung me and told me "don't be shocked when you see my face", he was preparing me. As he entered the house my stomach did a flip, I waited for him to enter the lounge and when he came through the door I looked at him and I realized it was far worse than I had expected. I started to well up with tears but I steadied myself as he asked me "do I look like a thug mum", I replied "no, you're still beautiful" as I smiled at him. "No, really mum, look at it" he said but I lied and told him "it's not as bad as I thought it would be". I gave him a bottle of "Bio-Oil" and told him to use this everyday as it would help his scar to fade and this seemed to reassure him. I went upstairs and sat on my bed with my face in my hands "oh my God" I thought, it was terrible, then I rose and looked in the mirror and told myself that this doesn't't matter, it's still Simon and it will fade with time. He had missed out on his much loved Christmas dinner so his dad made one for him, which he thoroughly enjoyed. Having missed out on most of his Christmas leave he was soon off to Hounslow Barracks. He purchased yet another car, a green Ford Mondeo, his best vehicle yet. He didn't pay much for it but it was a good clean car with a good engine, which he needed for the endless trips to and from camp. After a busy twelve months of vigorous training, life as a Soldier was pretty much a normal way of life.

Simon had always shared a dormitory with the other lads but one day his Sergeant told him he was to have a room of his own which meant that he had been given the honor of Senior amongst his group. He was absolutely made up with this proposal and he took it very seriously. I asked him shortly after this if he was doing his" Corporals" and he told me "only when I get back from Afghan." He bought himself tea, coffee and sugar canisters, he picked up his portable TV from home and I gave him a quilt set for his new room which he made a home from home. He enjoyed this time to himself and took his role completely seriously. This was a new side to Simon but he was still having fun with the lads as he needed to be part of the crowd. You couldn't take the comic out of Simon, it was him. One day, probably through boredom or mischievousness, he and a pal decided to play a trick on one of the lads. They gathered up his personal belongings and taped them to the outside of his locker, using a full roll of masking tape, to make sure it would take a long time to cut it off. They taped his playing cards, socks, boxer shorts and anything else they could find and then stood proudly for a photo. They received regular room inspections from their Sergeants and seniors.

The rooms had to be kept immaculate with their bed made perfectly and shoes lined up. They had to look pristine to pass the test, not one thing should be out of place. On one such occasion, as the Sergeant was making his rounds for room inspections, Simon stood to attention by the side of his bed and as the Sergeant approached his area, Simon suddenly grabbed his boots and flung them out of the open window then stood back to attention. When he saw what Simon had just done the Sergeant shouted "Annis, why have you thrown your boots out of the window?" Simon then said "Sir, because every time you inspect my locker, you do, Sir!" He said this whilst resisting the urge to laugh, well what could they say, and Simon was right he was only saving them the job of doing it themselves. He got a roasting for this but nothing else became of it as Simon wasn't cocky in his ways, he was a comedian and he meant no harm and they knew this.

He got on extremely well with his Corporals and Sergeants and often went out for a drink with them but he knew that while he was in work, they were his superiors and he would never try to take advantage, he knew his place. Simon sometimes pushed his luck a bit and when the lads were on camp, maximum respect was given to the higher order, such as Captains and Sergeant majors, when walking through camp, if they passed another higher Ranking Officer, they had to salute whilst passing them and say, loud and clear "Sir!" Simon saw these people not just as higher ranks, he saw them as the men they were normally and on numerous occasions he would forget himself and while passing he would salute and say " alright Sir". When he had passed them by, they would look back at him wondering if they had heard him correctly, but this was Simon, no malice just Simon being his natural self.

Many a time when he and his pals were allowed out of camp, they would go into Hounslow Centre where there was never a dull moment. On one occasion Simon was up to his usual tricks and he instructed his fellow pals to watch what he was about to do. They followed him and one lad used his mobile phone to video Simon as he entered the local supermarket. He continued up the escalator, very calmly, face blank as he picked up a large "two for one "offer sign. He casually put it under his arm, about turned and marched military fashion down the escalator amid laughs and cheers, as the on duty security guard watched him quizzically and with confusion. His eyes followed Simon until he reached the bottom of the escalator and then proceeded out of the large doors and into the car park where members of the public laughed and nudged each other. This is one of the many little antics that he got up to. Another time, he found himself a large cardboard box and put it over himself, he then crouched down and began to shuffle along the parade ground. When someone spotted this moving box, he would stop still and as he was completely hidden, it appeared that the box was moving by itself. All the time giggling could be heard from inside the box.

It was while Simon was still at Hounslow barracks that he carried out the battalions public duties, which involved him proudly standing guard outside the Royal Palaces, where crowds of people would pass by daily. He would stand in all his Blues, with rifle in hand, he was the proudest man there, so much had he achieved at such a young age. I am sad to say we let our boy down on this one as Simon had rung and asked if Pete and I could go down to London to see him at this proudest moment of his life. At the time, work commitments were a big pressure and we couldn't go. Sometimes memories come back to haunt people when they have lost someone and this is one of those times for us. Just to see mum and dad amongst the crowd would have meant so much to him, we let him down and that's something we have to sadly live with.

Butterflies and Feathers

Simon up to his old tricks

Always the Comedian

Coming of age

Doesn't life fly by so quickly? One doesn't realize at the time, but ten then twenty years will pass and we say "where did it go." One minute my little Dobber is holding on to me crying into my shoulder and now he's all grown up. Whilst Simon had been in Egypt he acquired the taste for scuba diving, his fear of water now a distant memory. The Army offered him a tour of Belize, to further develop his diving skills. He grasped this opportunity with both hands, it was a dream come true for him. He left for Belize in July 2008 where he had the time of his life and I am so glad he had this once in a life time opportunity. He managed to e-mail me and tell me "mum, you cannot imagine how beautiful it is here, if you and dad ever get the chance you both must come". He told me that the sea was so blue and clear and the pictures he took whilst diving were so awe inspiring.

Colourful fish of all shapes and sizes, corals of colours so beautiful, he called it paradise, one day he would go back, he told me. After looking at his pictures I was mesmerized at the beauty of the marine life, the closest I have been to this was when we had a fish tank many years ago. We had numerous tropical fish, but to see them in their natural environment is so special and so unforgettable.

Whilst in Belize, Simon had his 21st birthday, what a location to celebrate a milestone in his life. It was the perfect setting and it must have felt like one mesmerizing dream for Simon. One morning they were preparing for yet another training exercise and with kit and diving gear on board, they set off. A call came over the radio informing them that someone was in difficulties whilst diving. Simon immediately suited up and overboard he went to find the person in question. As he sank deeper into the water towards the sea bed, he noticed something glinting on the bed and as he approached he noticed a large bottle of champagne with a large 21st badge attached. I can imagine the delight in his eyes as he made his way to the surface with his gift, he was overwhelmed and totally surprised and what a perfect way to start his birthday. They partied all that night with Simon dressed in a grass skirt with his 21st badge pinned to his shirt.

Because Simon was always the cheeky character, he became friendly with a group of American tourists when in a bar and he managed to get them to buy him drinks all night. He learnt a lot on this tour and it was something he continued to talk about for months. He told me he was going back there but wasn't sure when that would be. He was there for three weeks before his return to the UK. He met many people on this tour and made some good friends, some he remained in contact with. Shortly after Simon's death, we received a letter from a kind lady named Sophie, who along with her husband Joe, and daughter Alex, knew Simon in Belize. Joe was the diving supervisor overlooking the trip and this is what she wrote:-

"We knew Simon for the briefest of moments, but he made a huge impression on all of us. What was to be an early night after our long journey, turned into a long one when we bumped into the lads as they celebrated Simon's 21st birthday. They were all dressed in Hawaiian skirts; Simon also had on a grass skirt and was covered in glow sticks. Around his neck was a large medallion made from string and a tin lid with the words "21 today" emblazoned on it, he was clearly enjoying himself. During our stay it was our privilege to spend our evenings in their company sitting on the beach, talking, laughing and joking. Simon was the life and soul of the bunch. Always smiling and happy, always something funny to say, a real character, a lovely lad. I remember one night in particular we were discussing where we all came from and our various accents, I can hear Simon's voice, in his broad northern tone, saying ; "I aint got an accent, me!" We all fell about the place. We will always remember him. As we left, it was so awful to think of those young lads going off to war, although I knew it was a possibility that some might not come home, I never really believed it and I cannot believe what's happened now. We grew very fond of them all but Simon most definitely shone; he was the star of the show, as I am sure he was wherever he went. I cannot imagine the dreadful pain you must be suffering, I am so sad and my heart aches for you all."

Ann Annis

Simons 21st in Belize, August 2008

Christmas 2008

Christmas 2008 was to be the last Christmas we would have the pleasure of spending with Simon. We did all the normal family things, big Christmas dinner; sometimes the turkey was so big that Pete had to kick it into the oven, where the top of it would touch the roof and burn. I remember many a disaster, trying to cook that perfect festive lunch and the ongoing joke about my turkey was that when we took it out of the oven, its legs were bald and the meat had shriveled up. It would look as if it had a jumper on, with sleeves rolled up. I was always scared to undercook it, so I made sure it always had that extra hour in the oven.

While we are on the subject of food, I must tell you of my fear when the children were little. I was always frightened of them choking so I would bite off the end of chips and anything sharp on their plates was removed and I only gave them soft crisps. I laugh now, especially when the children told me they didn't know for years that sausages actually came with crispy ends on. We would eat so much and then collapse in front of the TV and watch "It's a Wonderful Life". I remember the first time we sat our children down to watch this film and when seeing that it was in black and white, they moaned "aw mum, we don't have to watch this do we?" and my reply was "yes you will enjoy it" They sat and moaned for the first ten minutes then the room fell silent and they never took their eyes off the TV, until the film had finished. They enjoyed that film and watched it over and over again.

Isn't it funny, even after eating the largest Christmas dinner, the tin of chocolates came out less than an hour after? Pete and I always tried to make Christmas a happy and joyous time when the children were small. We would put them to bed early on Xmas Eve and while they supposedly slept, we decorated the home with balloons, tinsel, and Christmas decorations; it looked beautiful when we had finished and resembled a grotto. Then we would take the toys from their hiding places and assemble three piles, one for each of them, always making sure they looked the same size so when the children came down usually around five am, they couldn't compare. Just before we went to bed, exhausted, Pete would sneak up to their rooms and place a sock full of goodies on the end of their beds. In the morning, Pete and I would sneak downstairs to drink a cup of tea before the mayhem began. They would hear us and Pete would shout "He's been" then like a tribe of wildebeest, the children would climb over each other to come down the stairs. I loved to watch their little faces as they entered the lounge to the sight of the toy adorned decorated grotto. It was beautiful, the sight of children in awe filled my heart with happiness, and this is something that can never be replaced.

Then they would go to their own selected piles, Stuart would open his with a frenzy and not stop until all the surprises were unraveled, Natalie just plodded contently and Simon on the other hand, would slowly open one, then set to play with it, he would do this with each one, savoring each individual toy, it could sometimes take him hours to finally finish the unwrapping of all his gifts. The days when we sat and played Mouse Trap or Ker Plunk were the happier days, when as a family we got to do things together, sadly those times don't last long and as the children got older, computer games and mobile phones take over, which basically puts a stop to all interaction with the children as far as play goes.

When the boys were around ten and thirteen we bought them a Nintendo console and the game "Mario" came with it. We bought this in the October and put it away for the boys, but one night, I tried this game, just to see if it worked, which resulted in Pete and me getting totally addicted to it. Each night, with the children in bed, we drew the sofa up close to the TV and got out our supplies of crisps and chocolate in readiness for a full night of Mario. It took us well into December to conquer this game and I was devastated when we eventually finished it. Only after Christmas did the boys tell us they knew what they had been bought as they heard the music of the game each night and sometimes they would sit on the stairs, listening to our battles as we helped Mario on his quest.

Although the children were older, we still had a great Christmas. The Mouse Trap game was long gone by now and it was hard thinking what to buy for them. For Simon it was easy, amongst other things, I bought him a remote controlled helicopter, this was an indoor one and it was unbreakable. I thought he could take this back to camp but on its maiden voyage, he crashed it hard into the wall and this unbreakable helicopter broke, so we put it away to be mended. We also bought him a plastic gun, it fired foam rockets and it came with a target board, he loved this gift but sadly I had to confiscate it as the only delight he got from it was when he was shooting Mojo. He chased the poor dog all over the house, and then Mojo would turn and attack the rockets and try to eat them. It was chaos and I couldn't get the dog to calm down until the gun had been hidden.

It was at this Christmas that Simon challenged me to a poker game he bragged so much of how great he was at this, so I accepted his challenge. I bought Pete a small portable record player, I set it up then I dug all the records out that I hadn't heard for years and we played 70's and 80's music and Simon found out that he actually liked my taste in music. We cleared the coffee table and we all sat around with background music and tins of sweets as the game began. I knew Simon was a lucky card player but that night I was too, much to Simon's annoyance. We stayed up until 2.30 in the morning and in the end he had to admit defeat, he put my winning streak down to beginners luck and threatened to beat me the next time we played, sadly that time never came. What made it all very special is the fact that we had Simon to ourselves that night.

New Years Eve came and as usual we planned to go to the "Coach and Horses", which is our local pub, a place where everybody knows each other, a place where we knew we could relax amongst the company of friends without any trouble. We were to meet Pete's large family very rarely we saw the family so it was nice to catch up. Every New Year we would meet there, with our resident "Dj- Botty" and the landlord's curry to look forward to. Mattie was to meet us in there and we entered at 7.30pm as it was only a short stroll from home. The best side was filling up with people so we knew it was to be a good night. With dancing, poppers flying and laughter, the night was in full swing. For the first part of the night, Simon was unusually quiet, the tour of Afghanistan was drawing closer and I think this played on his mind but as time went by he started to cheer up with the help of a beer or two. Shortly after 10pm I noticed that Simon and Mattie had disappeared, in fact when I thought of it I hadn't seen them for a good 30 minutes. I was curious and about to go and look for them but as I got out of my chair, the pair appeared from out of the toilets, as bold as brass.

They walked back to their table, both with a smug grin on their face. Simon had a large red mark that stretched from one side of his face to the other, with a blotchy cheek bone, Mattie was slightly out of breath with a flushed face and marks down one side of his face. I knew immediately what this pair had been up to, they were always wrestling or toy fighting and this was one of those times. They had bumped into each other in the toilets and a wrestling match had broken out. To the unsuspecting public, this looked worse than what it was and as they entered the toilets they quickly turned and got out of there. Simon always marked easily, even with a little pinch, so after Mattie had finished with him he looked a mess. We had a fantastic night and it went off without any disturbance or trouble. It was late when we left and Simon was worse for wear so as he left the pub I was close behind him. He looked so childish and innocent when he had drink inside of him, always telling me how much he loved me. Simon would do absolutely anything that his dad and I asked of him, without complaint or answering back, nothing was too much trouble.

We gave him the nickname "Lurcio" (Royal Family) nothing was too much bother. When I came in from work he would say "Hello mother, do you want one of my super dooper coffees?" Although he let himself down with his untidiness and in every room of the home there was always something that Simon had left behind, what I would do now to have that mess back. Simon was the clumsiest person I had ever come across, he was always walking into things, chairs or anything in his path. Without fail every single time he came home, I could guarantee he would stub his toe on the living room door I could place a bet on it and win a fortune. He always opened the same door on his big toe, " stupid fat door" he would cry out in pain, hopping around on one leg with eyes watering but he never learned and did it over and over again. Simon's love for rapping was always present and when the song "The Boy Does Nothing "came out he would try and sing to this.

He was such a comical lad and it was lovely to have him home as it was so quiet without him. He was a considerate boy, so thoughtful and he always instinctively knew when Natalie was feeling down. He knew that she stressed a lot, always putting herself down and she had a lack of self-confidence. He made her feel better by saying "have you lost weight Tilly?" even though she hadn't but it made her feel better. When he saw me getting ready for a night out, he always said "you look lovely mum" and he made a point of going out of his way to say something nice, he was a proper softy. He would walk in boldly, noisily and the whole house would come to life. He could make me laugh when I was down, either by his March or salutes or by his outburst of singing.

I remember that last Christmas as if it were yesterday, a good Christmas had by all. Christmases from now on will never be the same.

2009

A new year was to begin, January 2009. The past twelve months had flown by so quickly, Simon had achieved so much and encountered things we could only imagine. He went back to Hounslow barracks to prepare for the inevitable tour of Afghanistan, which now had been brought forward from April to March. He didn't talk much about this to us as he knew it was part of his Soldier duties, guilty thoughts now linger in my mind, should I have enquired how he was feeling about the tour, did he worry. He didn't show any signs of stress and I didn't want him to think I was anxious.

Through January and February he encountered hard intense training. He made it home at weekends, still the same happy smiling Simon and on one of these weekends I remember Simon sitting crossed legged on the conservatory floor busy cleaning and polishing his ammo tin. He laughed when I asked him what they were for, " they hold the ammo mum" he proudly said , holding them up to the light to see if they were shining as well as they should be. "Why don't they just call them bullet tins or "BT's" for short," I asked him. He and Pete thought this hilarious "ok mum, I will tell my mates they're called "BT's from now on". He humoured me, smiling to himself as he got on with the job in hand.

The weeks passed by. It was one month before the onset of his tour and nothing had been said, no dreads, and no regrets on entering the Army. He went shopping and bought all the necessary kit he needed, gloves, thick socks, shaving creams and all the other personal effects to take with him. I saw all the things he had and thought that these bare necessities would be his only home comforts for the long six months away. His laptop would be of no use so far away in the barren place he was to vacate to. Up until early 2009 the situation in Afghanistan wasn't truly understood by me, I knew that heroes had sadly lost their lives but I didn't see much on the TV, so basically I have to admit I was ignorant as to the situation. I thought it was a tour they all had to experience, I never looked at it as a deadly bloody war it is today. Now, somewhere in the pit of my stomach, I had an unfamiliar feeling of dread.

We only had a few days left before our son had to leave so along with friends we all went out with Simon to give him a good send off. Late on at the local pub, I retreated to the quietness of the beer garden and I sat and cried, I was emotional and the vodkas didn't help the matter. An arm came across my shoulder Jason Reed (Reedy) had joined me. I broke down and confided in Reedy of my thoughts, the thoughts I hate to this day. I told him," I think something is going to happen to Simon", he told me " don't worry" but it was normal for me to worry, " No", I said " Listen and believe me when I say, mother's instinct is telling me this and I can't get the thought out of my head". He soothed me and tried to reassure me that this was normal but deep inside I knew and this feeling of dread never left me, every day, every minute and every second while Simon was away.

My bond with my son had been so close since the day I held him for the first time, my soul and his entwined. Stuart, our first born, had encountered action while he served in Iraq when just 18 years old and I worried, of course I did, but somehow this was completely different. I hated thinking these terrible painful thoughts but they wouldn't go away and I had no control over them, they burned inside of me constantly.

With the promises of parcels and letters to be sent regularly, I hugged my son, "please, be careful" I pleaded, "I will" he smiled and cheekily lifted that eyebrow of his to make me laugh. Pete hugged him "you wimp" Simon said with a thump to his arm, then he was gone and the house fell silent. Now it began, the countdown to his leave in June. He left for his tour of Afghanistan on 24th March 2009, the day of Pete's birthday, what were his thoughts, what were his fears, the kit he carried was so heavy and given the chance I would carry it for him. Landing in Afghanistan, a hostile unfamiliar place, did he remember all his training which was to prepare him for the task ahead and most importantly, to keep him safe?
Pete and I busied ourselves, we would send parcels galore, and anything he needed that would help went into these boxes. We often sent out two a week, everything went into them, chocolate, crisps, newspapers, toiletries, in fact, anything that we could get in with a squeeze.

We would watch TV to see if we could spot Simon, just to catch a comforting glimpse but we never did. Just one week after he had left us, we received our first of many phone calls. I could tell by his tone that he hated it, he had so far to go, so much to do, he was unusually quiet, conversation was all one sided. We chatted about the weather and work or what his sister was up to; obviously Simon couldn't talk about his work so conversation was strained. His joking manner had now left him and I sensed unhappiness but I knew he would eventually settle down and things would ease a bit when the teething troubles of settling in had passed. He had not yet received any parcels but it was early days, sometimes they could take weeks.

I wrote to him every week, it was difficult because the things I had written in the letters were often repeated during our conversations when he rang home. The hardest thing is that we never strayed far from the home phone for fear of missing his call. We couldn't ring him and what if he rang and there wasn't an answer, how would he feel, maybe that phone call home was the highlight of his day and if no one answered he would go back to his duties and have to wait another day before he got the chance to use the phone again. How would he feel, lonely, yes I think he would, they needed to hear voices from home, I think it helps to keep them going, especially if they are feeling down. I still carried that ache inside of me, that intense worry; I tried to put it to the back of my mind.

Another phone call came and by now I had memorized the all too familiar number on my phone. I would answer, then a pause as the call connected "Hello" he said quietly, it was hot, dry and dusty and he was finding it hard to adjust to these unfamiliar weather conditions when all I complained about was the rain. "I will swap you" he would say, as to feel the rain would be a much awaited treat. He longed for the feel of rain on his hot fatigued face and all I could ask him, on the subject of work, was "are you busy?" and always the same reply "Yes."

The day his first air mail letter dropped through the door, I hurriedly scooped it up, made a coffee, sat down making myself comfortable with no distractions. It was upsetting for me to read because I sensed he was writing it whist hiding his true emotions and thoughts. In it he says "don't worry about me, I'm keeping safe and sound and can't wait for the English weather, it's boiling here" I soon wrote back as the thought of him receiving no mail and watching his pals reading loving messages from home was something I couldn't bear so I wrote as often as I could and I also asked friends to write. In my letter I told him how all our fish had mysteriously died and it was only when Pete had gone to feed them one morning did he discovered the tragedy.

I told him how Nat and Nick were well and of all the gossip from around the town of Cadishead. The next letter he sent me was extremely moving and I could tell that he had matured and his attitude towards life was more of understanding. Simon wrote to us and said *"People out here actually want help, the way people live and survive here is so different to home you couldn't imagine".*

Within a few short months, war and destruction had already changed my son, his view on all walks of life was now changed, the words written in his letters were the only hint of his feelings that he ever showed me. In a phone call home he asked me to send him anything that could make eating pasta more desirable, he wasn't stationed in the main base but in a small outpost and the pictures that I had seen shocked me. The building they called Base, resembled that of a bombed out building, no windows or doors, derelict is the only word I can use about this shack. He had claimed his own corner and to make it more comfortable had adorned the bare brick walls with photos, flags and pictures. I sent him sachets of salt and pepper along with mayo and ketchup to flavour the pasta along with all varieties of dry goods that only required the use of hot water, to try and add variety to his dull tasteless diet. He actually told me that he and the lads had resorted to making their own bread on small camp fires within the walls of the camp. It's no wonder life was made all the more depressing, showering in cold water, eating dull foods day after day except of course when the lads received their much wanted parcels, containing home comforts, sent by their loved ones.

We sent him parcels, two or three a week, we would walk around Tesco with the open boxes in the trolley, placing everything in them and only stopping when we thought they were up to the required weight allowed for posting. Not to send him regular parcels would have devastated me, thinking that he would be waiting for them, to hurriedly take them to his room and rip them open excitedly. Having none for him and having to watch his pals open theirs while he sat alone with nothing, was unthinkable. It was not all doom and gloom, they did try to make the most of the situation, they played card games, on the rare occasions that they were allowed to take a bit of time to themselves, The game, much to Simon's delight was poker, this was his game. He could bluff and remain expressionless and he wrote that in one particular game he won 40 dollars. This game was a way to relax and to take their minds off the hard work ahead of them.

The phone calls began to reduce in number, fewer and fewer came our way as Simon found it harder to reach the phone or work commitments intensified. One day when the dreaded news broke that another poor soul had lost his life in the line of duty, the blackout of all calls home came and could last up to a week. During that time, not knowing if Simon was ok or how was he coping with the news was extremely hard, especially if we heard a tragic news flash on the TV. Our hearts sank but then we knew it wasn't our Simon as we would have already been told. "I can't do this anymore" I told Pete, Simon had been out there only two months and I couldn't stand it. I was becoming more and more depressed; I became moody and short tempered. I was close to cracking up but I tried to remain calm, "not long now to his R & R", I told myself.

We lived for his phone calls and every time he rang, I would sigh with relief that he was ok. "Hello mother, how are you all doing?" he quietly said, "Fine Dobber, how are you getting on?" I would chat for a while then pass the phone to Pete, for man talk. I slept that night but in the morning, a new day, the worry would begin all over again. I know that I come across all doom and gloom about the situation in Afghanistan and I have said that Simon didn't like it, he didn't, but he loved his job and with all jobs there is a down side and this was that down side. I didn't agree with the way he lived out there but nothing less than a four star hotel was good enough for my boy. I do realise they have a job to do and it isn't easy, but it doesn't help me, as a mother, to think this. I know he sometimes had a good laugh with his mates out there but I saw him lose weight and I didn't like it, I felt for him. I wanted him home so that I could see he was safe, it was the unpredictability of the place that frightened me.

Butterflies and Feathers

Simons letter home

Mum + Dad,

hiya, hope your both good, I'm ok just plodding along. Iv got both ov your packages thank you, sorry Iv not wrote or spoke to you much not really had much time to myself, the temps got alot hotter ere its up to 38°C but wen you have all your kit on its about 44°C boilen cant wait to feel the english weather again. We've had a outbreak ov D+V ere bout 30 peoples gone down with it, I'm lucky it hosent got me, bin playin poker this week at nite n iv won both ov the games winning me a total ov 40 Dollers 😊 got letter ov Eddy n Stuart now n a package of lynn and dennis could you tell them thanks and I'll write as soon as i can, Iv wrote tilly a seperate letter so if she hosent got it tell her its on its way. Is you and dad still eaten weight watcers lol bless. Iv not asked about mojo for awhile is he still alive. right im of theres work to be done, n dont worry bout im keep in safe and sound take care n I'll speak to you both Son

Love Dogger

Rest and relaxation

At last, the month I longed for was here, June 2009 and Simon was on his way home. We paced the floor and wore out the carpets and then with the same old familiar force, the door flew open, my boy now a man, walked into the house. He had altered so much in such a short time, the sparkle in his eyes had gone, his hair was bleached from the searing sun and he was thinner and gaunt looking. His chubby belly had gone, the jeans he once filled now hung loosely and his belt was pulled tighter with the extra notches he had made for the perfect fit. I swallowed down the lump in my throat and I hugged him but my eyes told the story.

The temperature in Afghanistan reached 38c but with kit on it reached 44c. He was longing to feel the cold and gloomy British weather again and was still waiting to feel the rain on his face. He didn't get the opportunity though as the weather actually warmed up, much to his disappointment. "Do you want a coffee?" he asked me, as he knew he was the only one who could make my coffee just as I liked it. We sat and chatted, I couldn't keep my eyes off him, and here was my son, safe and sound, home for two weeks, no worrying for two whole weeks. He had lost a lot of weight even though he had been eating but they made sure the lads got the right vitamins etc. Maybe he didn't eat enough, maybe the heat affected him. I know that the kit he wore was extremely heavy but he did look gaunt and tired and I don't like to look at the photos of him in this way.

He told stories that entertained us, he told about the mouse that taunted the lads, such a small animal to cause so many discontentment's in the camp. They valued their rations and guarded them well but this little mouse was causing mayhem, he was getting into the food each night and feasting on it and much to the annoyance of all the occupants of camp this mouse avoided them all and disappeared. They searched relentlessly and the mouse always got the better of them so Simon made a large sign, it said, "S.A.S *MOUSE, WANTED DEAD OR ALIVE*". Days past by and eventually this mouse got his comeuppance, at last he was captured.

Butterflies and Feathers

The lads gathered and made a make do raft of leaves and sticks; they then placed this *"S.A.S.MOUSE"* onto the raft and put it on the river. The lads lined the bank and saluted the mouse as it sailed down the river.

He told us the story of how a lot of the lads had contracted dysentery and having no toilets it wasn't a place to get such a terrible condition. They realised the cause of the outbreak when they discovered a dead cat in the water tank. Although these stories were all part of that life in Afghanistan he didn't complain or moan, anything that was connected to his job as a Soldier, he kept to himself. He didn't want to discuss the role he played while being deployed, he was a true professional and what happened at work stayed at work. Now he was home he took on the role of son again, never looking for compliments or sympathies. We didn't ask him questions and if he needed to talk, he knew he could without being prompted, although Natalie did ask one question while we sat in the garden under the warmth of the sun. Naively she asked "What are the bombs like" and all he said was "Loud". I could tell that this was all he was prepared to say, no tales of woe or bravery or loss of comrades, he kept that side to himself and we respected him for it, although I knew when he eventually finished this tour, I would encourage him to talk to me, for his own benefit rather than mine but for now I left it alone.

Simon soon made up for lost time, he caught up with Mattie for a much needed and well-earned beer, then went to see his cousin Eddie, who he had grown very close to. He thanked Mattie for his letters and the Easter egg that he had sent to him. The humorous letters he received from Eddie were much appreciated, he apologized to me for only sending a few letters, he much preferred to talk on the phone as his spelling was atrocious but I could read his writing, I was used to his grammar but I think he was embarrassed when writing to his friends. At home Simon couldn't wait for a hot bath and hot stodgy meals as living with pasta had taken its toll. He found it hard to finish a meal, now he couldn't even finish his favourite burger on a bun. He made the most of his leave, relaxing and having a few nights out and most importantly, catching up on his poker, playing on line on his lap top. He went shopping again now he was wiser as to what he needed whilst away. He went along to the casino with Reedy one afternoon, it was very late before they arrived home, not a word was spoken of how much they had won or in this case, how much they had lost. Whilst

Simon was away Reedy sent him poker magazines, perhaps he thought that he needed the helpful tips.

Simon kept up with his fitness on this short stay at home, running for miles, not wanting to lose the level he had already achieved. Home he came, breathless and sweaty, then in the bath he went, he then marched downstairs and sat on the kitchen floor. This meant only one thing, a haircut was needed, he would use Pete's clippers and without a mirror would shave off his hair down to a number one. I would always finish it off for him and I liked to aggravate him. I did this by pulling hard on his ears, drawing them away from his head to get behind them for a neat trim. I remember once, he shaved his head and left a thick line of hair from the back to the front, I told him he resembled a Mohican and I dragged him back to the kitchen to finish it off, the funny thing is, he would have actually gone outside like that.

He visited lots of places while he was home, Blackpool being one of these. He came home and told me he had been to see one of those seafront palm readers, which surprised me, because like me Simon was skeptical of these activities but he told me what she had said. Apparently she told him that a tall man in a long black coat was watching over him. "What does this mean?" he asked me and I commented that it could be his guardian angel. We laughed and said no more about this unknown spirit but I wondered myself who and what the meaning was to this, but whoever it was, it was certainly no guardian angel and if it were, where was he when Simon needed him? Two days before Simon had to leave; we were alone in the house. "You ok?" I asked him " yes mother" he acknowledged and got up from his chair as he sensed that I was about to ask him something, " Simon, please be careful out there, don't be a hero, watch your back" he turned and looked at me and quietly said, " I will mum, I am going to write letters to you all and none of you can open them, only open them if I don't come back but don't worry mum, I will make sure you and dad are looked after". I looked into his eyes; he avoided them and turned away, leaving me alone. I was speechless, he didn't want any more conversation, he had said what he needed to say, he didn't want to give me any inclination of the dangers he would encounter.

I was clueless as to what my Simon's role was whilst in Afghanistan and that's the way my considerate boy wanted it. Two weeks was not enough,

Butterflies and Feathers

it flew by and he was soon preparing to leave again. He was to go back to Hounslow first then on to Afghanistan, for the final 3 months of his tour. I wonder what dread he had in his mind as he prepared to leave, it must have been horrendous but he left with his head held high, without saying "I don't want to go back." Later that night after Simon had left us again, I noticed the little joke he had left behind for me. All my ornaments had been moved or swapped around to different places, he often did this to annoy me, I liked everything in its place and little things like this irritated me but Simon got his kicks from it. The two weeks he was home with us went too quickly and now he would be away for a further three months before the hated tour would be over with Simon safe at last. He remained in the country for a further three days after he left us and one night he rang me on my mobile as he wanted to say goodbye again. "Don't worry if I don't ring" he said, I told him again that we loved him and we were so proud of him, his reply was "I love you too". That was one of two phone calls he made, where he had made sure he told us he loved us. It's as if he had to tell us over and over again, to make sure we knew he meant it. It was only after Simon died that Mattie told us while Simon was home on his R&R, he confided in him and said he didn't think he would be coming home. Perhaps this was on his mind when he made these heart rendering calls, I wish to God I had known then!

We started to notice that the news was highlighting more stories of the events taking place in Afghanistan, things were heating up, it took on a new level and the situation was intensifying. That ache in my stomach worsened, I wanted the war to be over either by peace talks or ceasefire, anything that would halt the killings my son was out there. Each day that went by with no news meant he was still safe, Dobber will be home soon. A week after Simon arrived back in Afghanistan he rang and said that the nights were getting cold but the days still tortured them with the dry blistering heat. He stunned me when he said he was reading the Bible he said it was because he was sometimes bored, " it will do you no harm" I told him "it's really good in parts" he said. I felt sorry for him when he told me this, was he trying to distract himself, was he trying to keep away from the thoughts of what he had seen or was he looking for help by thinking "look God, I am reading your book, keep me safe" I cried at the thought of this.

Simons hunt for the rebel mouse and Simon in Afghanistan

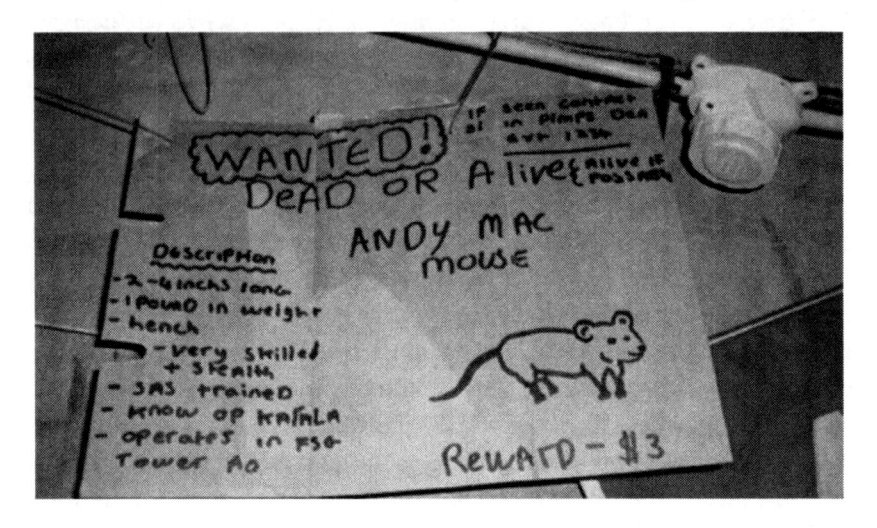

Butterflies and Feathers

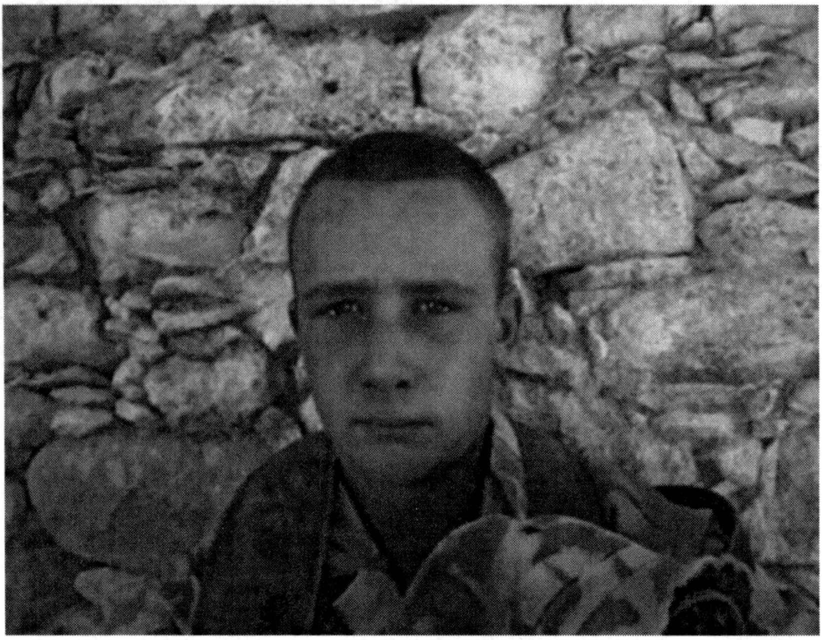

Death Valley, Sangin

July 19th 2009 was a sad day, a horrifying day, it was the day that Simon lost a true friend, Corporal Joey Etchells; he lost his life whilst out on foot patrol. We had met Joey only once, he was a mature, sensible beautiful boy, Simon and Joey had become close friends. Upon hearing the news my world came crashing down, now it was all too real. Before, it had happened to Soldiers we didn't know, the reality of the war now hit me. Simon couldn't ring as the block on the phone lines were now in place, how was he coping with this news when I wasn't there to comfort him in his sorrow and when I couldn't hear his words of grief.

"Was he sleeping, was he eating?" I couldn't bear the thought of him dealing with this news on his own. A soldier needs to follow the grieving process but sadly they have a job to do and they must get on with it.. I wrote him a letter, I didn't know what to say to make him feel better, no words could make the situation easier. He rang a few days after, he was extremely quiet, he didn't want to talk about Joey and I sensed the hurt in his voice. It cut through me, I couldn't help my son, I felt useless. He was now back on normal duties which personally I think was too soon. He was angry now and more determined to get on with the job, to fight for his pals and especially for Joey. It was in this phone call that he told me he and the lads didn't feel appreciated, they felt alone in the job they were doing and felt that people back home didn't care or just didn't want to know what they were all experiencing. I tried to tell him he was wrong and that the whole Country was right behind them, I told him again how we were so proud of him and I tried my best to make him feel a little better but I knew it didn't work. I have been told stories, after Simon left us for a better life, that when the troops in camp were down with morale at an all-time low, it was Simon who lifted their spirits even though he was hurting so much himself.

Simon's 22nd birthday on Sunday the 9th August was approaching and my little man had gone from being a mischievous little "Dennis the Menace" into a son that we were immensely proud of. We looked forward to watching him fulfill his dreams and live the full and rewarding life that was to come. Our job was done, we did our best and now it was up to him to find the right path in life. We sent another letter, we wished him a Happy Birthday and we expressed our sorrow for the loss of Joey.

Pete and I had booked a holiday the year before, for our Silver Wedding Anniversary, and saved hard for this. It was only the second holiday on our own without the company of our offspring. It was to be a cruise as we were both petrified of flying. We had flown before but never took to it and slowly the fear crept in and we felt that we just couldn't step on a plane again. It wasn't to be a luxury cruise, it was an economy Mediterranean cruise with an inside cabin, a fourteen night Mediterranean Medley departing from Southampton. "Fly mum its safe" Simon used to tell us, he tried endlessly to dispel the fear, the cruise was a safe bet, we could swim, we told him.

We sent enough parcels to keep him going while we were away but some of the letters, along with the parcels we had sent, came back to us unopened one day. One parcel held a birthday cake with candles along with banners, party hats and birthday badges. The other parcel held cards, chocolate, crisps and two photos that he had requested, one with Pete and I and the other of Natalie, as a reminder of the people who loved him and awaited his return.

It was Thursday August 13th when our son rang us, it was to be the last time I was to hear his soft and gentle voice. The call came late, around 9pm and I snatched up the phone. "Hello mother" he quietly said and I wished him a Happy Birthday, he had received some cards but not all, he had not received his birthday parcels and I cursed the delay as I had sent these parcels out at the end of July, to get there in time and they still hadn't arrived. My son woke up on the 9th August with nothing to open, damn the Army for this, I was livid with anger and resentment. He said it didn't matter but to me it did. Shortly after his death I asked a friend of Simon's, who had been at the same camp, "did Simon enjoy his birthday" The reply came back that Simon never mentioned his birthday, we didn't know".

Did he sit on his own this day? I told Simon that we were sorry we weren't there to celebrate with him but all he said was "are you ready for your holidays"i didn't tell him that I was dreading it, I didn't want to go, I even told my boss I didn't want to go "Why?" he asked "I don't know, I feel that something is going to happen" "Don't be daft, once you get there you will enjoy it, it will do you both good" but I didn't want to miss out on Simon's phone calls. We should be home to receive his calls, he might need us but the holiday was paid for, the bags packed and we assumed it would do us good. This last call was one of the hardest, most heartfelt conversations we had and I found it very emotional to talk with him.

The way he came across, his voice, his manner, "was he trying to tell me something" Images of Simon flashed through my mind, the altered face, thin, tired, homesick and I broke down, which was something I hadn't done in his presence before, " I love you, please be careful" I handed the phone to Pete hoping that Simon hadn't picked up on my sadness, I left the room and sobbed my eyes out, "why had this conversation been like this?", the other calls had not ended this way, it was a very sad and emotional good bye. Pete said "try and ring on the 29th August, we will be home then" and as he hung up, we exchanged glances, no words were spoken, we both heard the worry in our son's voice. The news on the TV told the story, Simon didn't have to mention the situation in Afghanistan, it was extremely hostile and he was working long hours on foot patrols.

Friday 14th August, the eve of our holiday departure, we quietly went through all the necessary holiday checks, money, suitcase labels, the car filled with petrol ready for the long journey to Southampton. I left post-it notes for Natalie saying "water the plants" "feed Mojo at six pm" "bring in the milk" and so on. I longed for just one more phone call from Simon but it didn't come. I had a restless sleep that night.

Saturday 15th August, we loaded the suitcases into the car, we should have been relaxed, happy in the anticipation of the adventure ahead of us but we were not, we were both tense and moody. I still felt that never ending ache inside of me, that feeling of worry and anxiety. I was hoping once again for that last phone call before we set of but this didn't come either. We set off early for the five hour drive to Southampton, we were finally getting that holiday we yearned for but the atmosphere was odd, one would think we were on our way to boot camp rather than a cruise around the Mediterranean.

We listened to CD's, ate sweets and chatted mundanely but halfway through the journey I put on a CD that I had found in the glove compartment and halfway through the song, I heard the line, "Soldiers marching through the night" and suddenly a dread passed through me and I shuddered, I couldn't stop thinking about Simon. Then to make matters worse, Simon's favourite artist Eminem, came on. In hindsight we should have listened to our hearts and turned the car around because since he went away on tour, I hadn't felt right.

We finally arrived at our destination, a large secure car park, where we were to leave the car whilst we cruised. We loaded our cases onto the shuttle bus and within half an hour we set off to the port. As we stepped off the bus minus our cases, which were to be sent to our cabin, we were mesmerised by the sight of our ship. The Grand Princess, she was enormous, this I didn't expect having only travelled on a ferry in the past,. The crew was friendly and as we boarded they went through all the checks and procedures, they gave us our room key and we stepped onto the ship.

This beautiful, magnificent vessel surrounded with lavish ornamental balconies, with plush carpets and extravagant duty free shops. For an instant all my worries subsided with the sight of splendor that surrounded us, we did deserve this, we worked and saved so hard for this treat and we hurriedly walked to our cabin, which took a while to find. The ship was vast with walkways leading off in all directions and we were located on dolphin deck. The balcony rooms were the best accommodation and they were located at the top but we didn't mind, we were happy without a balcony as we wouldn't be sat in it all the time. Upon entering our cabin we were surprised at just how big it was with double bed, wardrobes and a nice little bathroom with shower, it was lovely. Pete wanted to leave the cases and go explore the beauty of the ship but I had to have everything perfectly placed then I could relax so we steadily unpacked our cases, changed and then we went to explore.

On the cruise we were to explore many different locations, the first being Gibraltar, then Cadiz and Cannes and many more. I wanted to relish each and every one of these places and I wanted to explore the different life styles, to sightsee all their heritages. It was only three pm and the ship was set to sail at five pm so we excitedly made our way up to the top deck as the view from up there was amazing, we were so high up. The restaurants and snack bars were now open and these were free to us so we made the most of them and sat down to eat. I was going to make the most of these

Butterflies and Feathers

freebies but unfortunately alcohol wasn't on the free list so we bought a much needed drink, as after the long drive here we were both feeling fatigued. We sat and waited for the ship to sail so that we could look at the scenery as we left our cold, rainy country.

My worries over Simon had eased a bit now and I was relaxed, although my lovely boy never left my thoughts. As the engines from this large vessel kicked into life, the rumble shuddered through the ship, turbines bringing this huge floating village to life as slowly she began to move, barely altering the sea's surface, so slow, so graceful, the only hint of her movement was the disturbance in the water below. I became disoriented, were we now sitting at the front or were we at the back, Pete laughed at me, I never did have a sense of direction. He walked me around the upper decks to give me an idea as to where we were, we explored our surroundings, bars showered the place with eating stations in convenient places, and there was no chance of going hungry. Small swimming pools to soak up the sun, too many to count and in the middle of the ship, a large outdoor TV screen where we could sit watching a matinee under the stars and a large crowd had already gathered to watch the football. From the top deck, we watched the rugged coast of Britain fade away into the distance, we were now gathering speed and the white crested waves so strong and forceful were lashing the sides of the ship as she sliced through the surface leaving an unsettled froth in her wake. I felt safe on this vessel, I liked it instantly.

We entered the restaurant, having only snacked before and spoilt ourselves with the vast amount of mouthwatering food that was on offer. It was cold outside, especially with the breeze coming off the cold sea but we knew that once we entered our first stop of Gibraltar on Tuesday morning that the weather would alter and the heat of the sun would hopefully grace us and then we could make use of the tempting water of the pools.

By 7pm we had endeavored to find and test each little bar, this was lovely; we had a full fourteen days to take all of this in. Tiredness now caught up with us, so we retired to the cosines of our cabin. Upon inspection of his phone, Pete realized he had a missed call off Stuart, we couldn't return the call as the signal was very poor now, it would wait until tomorrow, we didn't worry too much as he probably wanted to wish us a good holiday as we hadn't seen him before we left. We watched the TV and surprisingly we both fell fast asleep. I couldn't hear the roar of the engines or feel the rocking of the ship as it made haste through the Bay of Biscay.

Sunday 16th August 2009 was the day that my soul was torn in two. We awoke early, fresh and ready for the first full day of our holiday. We quickly dressed and went for breakfast, the ship was full of holiday makers, children chasing each other excitably, the weather was still cool and breezy, and we were amazed at the abundance of the breakfast food. I tried to be posh and ate croissants accompanied with freshly squeezed orange juice, and then I got bored with my selection and settled for a full English breakfast instead. We strolled along the deck, still attired in jumpers and I yearned to feel the warmth of the sun but I wanted to stay out of the cabin as it was small and cosy but had no windows so we had no concept of moving. We came across a journey log on a digital screen, highlighting our progress, so far out to sea now, so far away from home.

We sat and chatted a while to others, the bars had opened and everyone was already in a merry holiday mood. We visited the casino, a place unfamiliar to me, "one for Simon" Pete said, "I hope we have his luck". We set a budget of £10 each, no more, no less, that was to be our limit. I played a card game, I can't say what it was but I lost within minutes, then slowly I won and eventually I gained my £10 back, so I stopped as I found it all pointless. Pete on the other hand, won £20 but we didn't push our luck, we stopped there and Pete took the chips to save for another day. Back at the front of the ship, or was it the back, I didn't know as I was still confused, there was an opening show to welcome all guests aboard, there was singing, with an accompanying band and we enjoyed it. They announced the Captain's Ball for that night and anyone could attend, as long as they adhered to the correct dress code as it was in the presence of the Captain! I had brought a posh frock along with me, but we couldn't decide if we wanted to attend as it wasn't really Pete's thing and his suit normally came out for funerals or weddings.

We filled the afternoon by exploring the ship, finding every nook and cranny then we ate again. Lunch was a buffet style menu, I had to taste a bit of everything, we were so spoilt for choice and after a few drinks I was exhausted, I had eaten far too much and now I needed a siesta. On the way back to the cabin, I noticed crowds of people hurrying to the side rails so we followed them wondering what they were pointing at out at sea. I heard happy voices shouting "Look, over there, dolphins". I saw my first dolphin in the wild as they swam in uniform, swift and elegant through the water, maybe they wanted to out swim the ship or were they just saying "Hello". We took our drinks back to the cabin, flopped on the bed to watch TV, swearing to pace ourselves from now on and not to overindulge.

Quickly we were both sound asleep. It was four pm when the sound of the phone woke us, we both sat up quickly, rubbing our eyes, looking to where the noise was coming from. We looked quizzically at each other as the ringing stopped. Had we ordered room service, I couldn't remember, then it startled me as it started ringing for the second time. I slowly got up and made my way over to phone, "Hello" I answered, "The Captain would like to speak to you and your husband, this is Mrs. Annis isn't it?" the unknown lady said. "Yes it is" I replied, "He is on his way" she politely said and then she hung up. I looked at Pete and said "the Captain's on his way" I felt a flush raise up to my face, my stomach started to churn, "why?" Pete asked, "Its Simon" I told him. "Why else would the Captain feel the need to visit us?" I hurried over and sat close to Pete, we both sat perfectly still, we didn't speak as we stared at the door anxiously awaiting our visitors.

Five minutes felt more like five hours and the tap on the door snapped us back to reality. Another tap, I looked at Pete but he wasn't moving so I got to my feet and slowly opened the cabin door. Peter's pale face looked on as three strangers walked slowly in. It was the Captain who I knew from his badge and two others whom I didn't know. Their heads were lowered and we knew then as their manner gave it away. I turned and went to Peter's side, we found each other's hands and held on tightly to each other. I will never forget the words that followed.

The Captain looked at us, he stalled uneasily, then said quietly "Have you a son in Afghanistan called Simon Annis" We nodded, "I am so sorry" he said. We both stared pleadingly at him, tears rolling down our faces, "Is he wounded" I asked. "Sorry no, he has been killed" He was finding the words hard to say, I felt Pete trembling and that ache I had held for so many months finally erupted. "No, he is injured Pete, they have got it wrong, tell us you have it wrong, he is injured" I cried, "Sorry" came the reply. Pete broke down and I grabbed hold of him, "He promised me he wouldn't die, he promised" Pete shouted hysterically, my mind sent images, flashing in front of my eyes, I was dizzy and numb, my mind chaotic with thoughts, Simon's face, Simon's life, Simon's still body too far away from me to hold and comfort. I couldn't help Pete, I didn't know what to do, my strong loving husband now a wreck. I was scared, I needed Pete, but he needed me more, I had to stay strong.

I shook violently; my mind whirling out of control, my sweet darling, my dear beautiful son, dead, those words repeated in my mind, "Simon's dead, Simon's dead". We both sobbed and held each other tightly, my stomach hurt, a strange hurt, a feeling that in all my long life I had never felt before. This cannot happen to us, to Simon, "Pete, what are we going to do," I cried into his shoulder " I don't know" he wept, the feeling of utter helplessness swept over us, we felt small and isolated, alone and frightened.

We had spoken to him on Thursday and I tried to remember the sound of his voice and I couldn't. That cute new born I had held in my arms twenty two years ago, so young, he had so much to live for, so much love. We resembled zombies, unmoving, starry eyed, in shock, we longed for Simon, we hurt so much, " Simon's dead," in my mind over and over, it wouldn't go, "Simon's dead" it wasn't real, he was careful, he told me that. They gave us a cup of tea, as if that would ease the pain and anguish, my shaking hand let go of it. From that day, from that hateful hour, we changed, our personalities, our outlook of this cruel unfair world, we changed in an instant.

While we were sleeping in our snug warm bed, while we ate and drank, our caring son had been on foot patrol, he had died so far away, on his own. I couldn't comfort him or be there to listen to his dying words, to look into his blue eyes and stroke his head; he lay on his own, thousands of miles away, away from us, away from those who loved him more than life itself. Haunted images again flashed through my tormented mind, was he aware he was about to die, did he open his eyes to look at the horrendous injuries he suffered, was he frightened, did he cry out in fear or were his last words. "Please help me." "What are we going to do Pete, please tell me" I repeated over and over again.

Pete was destroyed, I wanted to help but I didn't know how. We couldn't find the words to soothe each other. Lost in thought, I could see my son marching around the home reciting his number *"25225641, SIR"* and saluting. I felt the touch of his hand irritatingly ruffling my hair; I could feel Simon's pain. I sensed him reaching out to us, I heard his voice in my mind "Sorry mum" I answered him, "Sorry for what, silly, we love you, we will be ok" I lied. If only he could hear me. I couldn't bear the thought that he was sad or worrying about us. Simon's dead, that image again cut through my thoughts. Please let there be another place, safe, warm and comforting.

"How did he die?" I asked the Captain, I needed to know, but he couldn't answer that "what time?" "In the early hours of this morning" he said, "so why the hell had it took this long to tell us" I shouted but he couldn't answer that question either. They left us alone for a short while, we cried, we didn't speak to each other, and both our thoughts were with Simon. What the hell had he gone through minutes before his murder, was he tired, hungry or cold, "he promised me" Pete cried, "Simon can't be dead". The Captain came back and handed us a piece of paper with a phone number written on it, it was that of an Officer and we had to ring him to confirm that this horrific news had been broken to us. We knew that we had to ring this number but it was a long time before we did, this would be yet more confirmation that we didn't want to hear.

After an hour Pete picked up the phone and rang him, he was offered condolences and sympathies over our son. "A brave soldier" he said and suddenly a thought hit me "Oh my god, Pete, what about Natalie?" I cried. She was alone at home, how do we break the news to the sister who worshipped her big brother, we should be there at home amongst the family. Pete gathered his thoughts, steadied himself and tried to sound strong and picked up the phone. I lay on the bed with my face in a pillow, how can this be happening to us, we are a good decent family, we have tried to do everything right in our lives, why had Simon been punished, mummies little soldier was gone; it felt like a bad dream. Pete spoke quietly on the phone, tears streaming down his face, the hand that held the receiver shaking uncontrollably.

After he had spoken to Natalie, he sat down and crying he said "she knew, she sounded ok, the Police and Army came to her just before we were told, she was on her own at home, she saw them walk slowly up the garden path, she said she knew what they were there for, they went for Nick at work, immediately. Natalie was 19yrs old, she is a remarkable young woman, she took the role of mum and kept herself composed as she carried out the terrible task of informing the family. Shortly after, a text came through on my mobile, *"Mum, don't worry, I am fine, I am sorting things out here, love you xxx"*. She was a tower of strength, she was in shock and would not renounce her duties until we arrived home, then she would be allowed to grieve for her Dobber.

The news had already started to leak back home; Natalie had the press and TV at the door, which she promptly sent away, so much to deal with at such a young age. We needed to get home, the Captain visited us and informed us they were doing everything they could and that they were trying their up most to get us home quickly but eventually we were told we would have to stay on the ship until Tuesday morning when we docked at Gibraltar. They had tried everything but we were too far out at sea, every other port would take longer to get to now. I sat on the edge of the bed with Pete, staring into space for hours, lost in thought, we had to endure this for the next 48 hours, confined, avoiding people, poor Simon ,dead, that thought again, we both felt sick, numb and utterly lost. We were alone on this huge vessel, surrounded by water and if it wasn't for the knowledge of our two children waiting eagerly for our return, we could have easily jumped overboard. Life was now incomplete, we had three children, it was always, Stuart, Natalie and Simon, he is our son, still is, even though he isn't here with us.

We couldn't stand the confines of the cabin any longer, we were going crazy with anger and sadness, we needed fresh air so we rinsed our faces with cold water and sheepishly left the cabin, avoiding people and their faces, both our heads down, eyes fixed on the floor. We held hands tightly and made our way up to the top deck, it was around 9pm and the place was heaving with partying holiday makers, we hurriedly bought drinks, doubles, and found a quiet part of the ship away from human contact. We sat and looked out to sea, the dark clear night, the sea lashing up the sides of the ship, the sky clear and the stars plentiful. I looked up, found the brightest, largest star "are you there Simon, are you looking at this star with me?" "Yes" he answered in my thoughts; tears flowed down our cheeks as people passed by, not knowing of our pain.

I heard them laughing and joking with each other and I hated them all for their happiness, they had no idea that another young Soldier has suffered to make the lives of people in their Country safer. I wanted to announce it on the large outdoor TV screen, they had no right to smile or to be happy, "all of you think of my son! " I wanted to shout. Pete squeezed my hand tightly as another bout of loss and pain came over him, another image of his treasured son flashed through his mind. We drank double after double, it didn't have any effect on us, it just numbed us and we had to endure another day of this torment tomorrow.

Two weeks before the start of this cruise we had received a call from the Cruise Company offering us a great deal for 2010 if we cancelled, with a full refund. They obviously had a queue of people waiting for a cancellation and then I remembered the conversation I had with Reedy back in February and then the sad phone call from Simon on Thursday, the CD's and the constant thoughts of Simon on the way down, all this should have warned me not to come on this cruise. "Damn, I should have listened to my thoughts." Then to top it all I thought of the missed call we had off Stuart on the Saturday when we arrived. It was to tell us that another of Simon's friends had also lost his life this poor lad was also named Simon. I think that if we had answered that call, we would have definitely come home, all those poor mothers, their anguish so unbearable. Poor Simon, one so young to lose so many of his friends and he had to go on foot patrol in the early hours, shortly after this sad loss, it must have felt like hell had closed in on them. Wouldn't the world be a safe and better place if we all acted on our intuitions, it's always too late. I chose to ignore all these warnings and I am not superstitious but in the future I will give such matters a second thought.

Time stood still, we sat watching the sea in all its prowess, we cried and deep in our thoughts there were unanswered questions, we needed to be home and consequently we drank more but it did nothing to dull the ache inside us. My stomach churned over and over, we kept our heads low when people passed us by and I looked at the happy families, they seemed to not have a care in the world, no worries and with their families complete, I resented them all. Around 11pm we made our way, with drinks in hand , to the cabin, the ship was quieter now and the corridors empty, people tucked away in their beds dreaming sweetly of their next day's adventure. The cabin felt smaller and claustrophobic now, we put Cartoon Network on the TV to kill the silence, trying to distract ourselves from our thoughts. We both sat on the edge of the bed but after 30minutes we were pacing the tiny floor, we couldn't settle so we made our way up to the deck again, where we sat until 5am. The ship was deserted; a few cleaners hurried about their duties, the odd glances they gave us only worsened my anger. Again we went back to our cabin, we both lay down, Pete lay on his side with his back to me and I felt his shoulders moving as he quietly wept for his lad, I stroked his head and he drifted off to sleep. I lay there, the sobbing that came from Pete even in his sleep tormented me so much, and I didn't think I could carry on. I drifted in and out of sleep but dreams of my Simon woke me up so I lay next to Pete, watching him sleep restlessly. He woke less than an hour later and when he did, he just lay there with staring eyes.

At 8am, Kath, the Captains Aid, came to see us, they were sorting everything out, flights home, taxis, payments, and we needn't worry about anything. Our mobile phones kicked into life, the signals now strong, text after text came through, and messages from friends back home, sending their condolences and sympathies. It was heartfelt, the lovely sensitive messages they sent made us feel less isolated. Reedy rang Pete; I was relieved as he needed to talk about his feelings. We couldn't talk to each other as we were frightened to upset one another. Pete was like a ticking time bomb and he needed a release. I really don't know how we got through that day. I can't really remember what we did on Monday 17th August, it was all a blur but I do remember praying for the first time in my life. I prayed to God, I prayed he would make it all a mistake and Simon would be found safe and well and that there had been a mix up with his dog tags and he had actually been captured. This was the wish that stayed with me for months after and I often dreamt there was a knock on the door and when I went to open it, Army personnel were standing there to tell me that Simon had been found safe and well, it was all a case of mistaken identity and then he would bound through the door, apologising for being late. If only wishes came true.

Finally Tuesday morning arrived, we had been sat quietly waiting with our bags packed since 4am, we both showered and dressed and sat, we both looked dreadful, we were pale and our eyes were red rimmed with black shadows under them. I said to Pete "we had to be strong for the two children waiting for us, we won't break down when we enter our home, we must allow Natalie to be herself, to grieve for her brother without the weight of worry on her shoulders for her parents, we must be a rock for them". The ship was to dock at Gibraltar, it was 6.30 am and we went to see if it was nearing its destination. The heat hit us as soon as we climbed the stairs to the top deck, if it had been under different circumstances I would have looked at Gibraltar and gasped at its beauty but now it was nothing but a large rock that we needed to by-pass to get home.

We went back down stairs and the crew arrived at 7am to escort us off the ship. A Chaperone had been sent to escort us all the way back home to Manchester. As we walked away from our holiday we had our heads bowed down and were unable to look at anyone. The curious looks we received, from the tourists, started to unnerve me. A taxi had been booked and was waiting to take us to Malaga airport, a long and tedious drive that took maybe an hour or more. I'm not sure how long as we were lost in our thoughts but the journey was quiet. As we arrived at Malaga Airport the Chaperone collected the tickets, it was so busy, crowds of people queued for their flights dressed in shorts and sunhats with children crying in their buggies due to the heat and tiredness. We didn't have to wait long before we were aboard the large plane for the final leg of our journey. We had been warned beforehand that the story had broken in the UK, we were fuming, could they not wait until we were back, didn't they have the decency to let us get home first. Simon's picture was now in the papers, his face was now national, it made it all too hard to bear, it made it all too real, he was just another name, another way to sell their papers. We found ourselves looking at every passing person with a newspaper, thinking "do they know our boy now, our so laid back cheeky son or was he just a story, a statistic". The plane gained height and we were now truly on our way home, to a life that wouldn't be the same, so hollow and empty for the rest of our lives.

Across the aisle from Pete, a male passenger was intently reading the front page of his newspaper; Pete angrily snapped and snatched the paper from him. Simon wasn't on this front page and the man looked angrily at Pete so I apologised to him with no offer of explanation. I tried to soothe Pete and the Air Hostess offered us a drink, "vodka," I told her, I needed it and more. Pete offered payment but she refused, "no charge, it's from the Captain", this made me cry again. I quickly wiped away my tears, be strong, I told myself, from now on we have to appear strong. We hated flying, that's why the cruise appealed to us. Simon was forever saying "go by plane mum, you will be ok, it's safe" and now he had his own way. Here we were, many thousands of feet up, and we didn't give it a second thought, we couldn't have cared less if it had dropped from the sky, we half wished it would, it was nothing compared to what Simon had endured.

The plane finally landed at Manchester Airport, my stomach took a lunge, my head hurt and I wanted to cry but I held it in as I swallowed against the lump in my throat. The passengers were told to remain in their seats so they could take us off first and as we waited for the hatch to open, all enquiring eyes were set on us and as the door slowly opened my legs nearly gave way I took a sharp breath and stepped back as the two Padres came into view from the other side of the open door, they were there to receive and greet us," God no" I said, as the reality of what had happened to Simon hit us in the face. Tears were welling up inside of me again, "I can't", I whispered to Pete, "I can't do this" but he took my hand and we followed the Padres to collect our luggage.

We queued behind passengers, crowding the conveyer belt eager to collect their bags and make haste home but I wanted to get out, too many people, it was all too much. Before, we had managed to avoid crowds and now we were amongst a huge throng and I felt I couldn't breath so I found a chair to sit on as I needed to compose myself. We waited 30 minutes before our luggage came into view, it travelled slowly down the conveyor belt towards us, Pete hastily collected our cases then hurried to the doors, where the Padres handed us over to a high ranking Army Officer and his driver. We shook hands and he introduced himself, I will just call him" Colonel", he offered us his condolences then Pete and I quietly followed him to his car. We said goodbye to our Chaperone and thanked her for accompanying us, it felt like we had been out of the country for months, everything looked so different now.

Only four days previously we had left our home and to an extent, life was normal, but now that we were returning it was different, it was as if we had travelled into a different era from a different life into a new unfamiliar one, it was odd and strange, it was incomplete. I dreaded walking into our home, I didn't want to be there now, I didn't want to face up to the nightmare that awaited us, I looked at Pete and he gave me a strained weak smile. As we drove down our road, which once was welcoming, we noticed strange cars and people sat in them, they were TV and Radio crews, waiting for our return. I lowered my head as we passed them; we hurriedly got out of the car and entered our home. I couldn't read Natalie's emotions, she was so strong and dignified and along with Stuart, had maintained their composure but I couldn't help but notice that Natalie was in denial. The visiting officer, Major Mike, was already there and had been since Natalie had been told the devastating news; he was a tower of strength and professional in his job. All the downstairs rooms in our home were full of cards and flowers, extra vases had been bought to accommodate the beautiful bouquets that had been sent daily to the house, every gap was filled to the brim with cards and messages and vases, the scent of blossoms filled the air.

It was then that the questions, that needed answers, were asked. We were told that in the early hours of August 16th 2009, Simon had been on foot patrol in Sangin, when an I.E.D had gone off, the night was rocked and the silence had been broken when the I.E.D had been detonated. As the dust cloud slowly settled, they realized that there was a casualty; it was Simon's true good friend lance Corporal James Fullerton. All hell had broken loose. We were told little at this point as all they could say was that Simon went to James to administer First Aid to his pal. When he was placed onto the stretcher for evacuation, Simon lifted it with comrade Louis Carter and along with two others they made their way onwards. Simon had tragically stood on another of these murderous I.E.D's and all three brave Heroes lost their lives in the same tragic explosion. My mind couldn't take all this in, I needed to know one thing, "did Simon suffer, did he die instantly?"I demanded to know.

They told me what I wanted to hear, what I needed to hear that" yes he did". I know they couldn't have known this answer and I knew it was for my benefit and I wouldn't know the truth until the inquest, which would be many months from now. I made myself believe what they told me, for now but I needed to know the fear he felt. He knew his job and he did it well but it came with the knowledge that it could result in death. Did he think this that fateful day, when he ran to help his loyal friend? I tried to imagine this pain of his, I wish I knew all the answers and worst of all did he speak in his dying moments, was he alone, will we ever know?

People were at the door again, I know they meant well but we couldn't face anyone, the cards and messages flowed in by the hundreds, flowers took over every spare inch of the house. I felt I was living a bad dream, only with dreams we wake up and all the bad things go away but this time I couldn't wake myself, I was living this dream. We didn't watch TV, it remained unplugged, everything on it was a reminder. News stories of Afghanistan filled the headlines as more and more Soldiers lost their lives or succumbed to horrific injuries. The radio also remained silent as we wanted no contact with the outside world, we wanted to remain isolated in our home, me especially, it got so bad that I couldn't go out. I remember the day I actually went alone to the local Tesco, it was horrendous, I had to get out of there, I ignored people I knew for fear they would talk to me. Even now, twelve months on, I'm not happy and confident going out alone.

Shortly after our arrival home, Pete's large family came to visit, so many people were crowded into our home, we sat chatting and the many stories of Simon filled the air. As I sat quietly taking all this in, I found myself counting heads, it was strange, there was a gap in numbers, someone was missing so I placed family members with family members and re-counted, "who's missing?" I thought. It was my son, Simon, he was missing, the chair he normally sat in whilst he picked on my vase full of reeds, was now occupied with a family member, it was odd not to see him there, he had such a huge presence and that night there was truly a large hole where he should have been. I became very angry with everyone and if someone came to the door that had not seen Simon on a regular basis, I sent them away. "What right had they to knock on my door, where were they before?" if these people had sent my son letters while he was in Afghanistan, he would have been overwhelmed with the amount of support shown for him but all this was my anger surfacing. I know that now but it took a long time to see it and get over that phase of my grief. The conversation I had with Simon, when he expressed his concerns at the lack of support, made me all the angrier and in a way, he was absolutely right. At the time, the media coverage didn't show the whole extent of the war as we know it today; it's a shame that it takes a lot of deaths to bring all this to light. Right from the start there should have been full coverage, every step of the way and when I hear of another fallen Soldier whose story doesn't get reported first on the news and is placed behind gossip about a celebrity who has divorced or something mundane like that, I get so upset, because it isn't right.

As the days went by, Peter and I survived on a few hours' sleep a night, we drank more and more as it helped us sleep and we could only nod off if the TV was on in the background. If the bedroom was quiet, the tormented images came and we both went downstairs in the early hours of the morning. I started to hear Natalie cry at night when she thought we couldn't hear her, when she was alone with Nick. She had started to deteriorate since our return. Pete and I couldn't talk to Natalie about Simon as it hurt us and we couldn't find the words needed to console each other. I would find Pete many a time, lying face down on our bed, eyes and cheeks wet with tears but I wouldn't talk to him, I silently cuddled him as I couldn't find the words that would make him feel any better, there were none.

Repatriation

Simon died on 16th August 2009 and he was to be repatriated to the UK through RAF Lyneham, his body was to be released into the jurisdiction of HM County Coroner for Wiltshire. Then he was to travel through the thoughtful little town of Wootton Bassett, along with three other heroes. We were never left alone, the home was full with Simon's friends or family members, our VO Major Mike was constantly by our side, he took all the worries off our shoulders and anything we needed he took care of. At first we wanted to sell our house, the memories in the home haunted me; Simon was everywhere, in the garden with his ants, sitting on the kitchen floor shaving his head, his bedroom where he spent twenty two years of his life. I wanted out, but as time went on, I needed these treasured memories, and I wouldn't move, Simon was no longer here but his presence was, in all his entirety.

The journey to RAF Lyneham was long and tedious, yet another hurdle to conquor, our son was coming home, the last time he was on the plane, he walked on and nothing in the world could have prepared us for this. Now he was to be carried off in a flag covered coffin, it all seemed too final. They said Simon was the 201st Soldier to die in Afghanistan and as I sit here now, the total is over 300. It's safe to say that the majority have lost their lives through I.E.Ds, a hidden killer. This is a war where we cannot see the enemy, do they stand a chance, "I wonder?"

It was August 21st and the families of the other three lads were there to receive their sons, it was somber, the weather was dull and cloudy, the silence was overwhelming as we stood and watched the unclear sky, all families now united in grief. I felt Simon was near now, my stomach churned with butterflies as the realization hit me. Before, I thought I had felt his presence but standing there on that airstrip I felt a pull inside me, an overwhelming feeling that I cannot describe but it grew stronger as my son travelled nearer. We waited to hear the giant engines of the Hercules plane, the giant grey troop carrier, now empty apart from four flag draped coffins and their Chaperones. Before their departure from Afghanistan, the troops had a moving memorial, to pay their last respects and give prayers for their lost brothers in war. The escorts that accompanied the coffin were never to leave its side, they were given the respect that a hero justly deserves.

All the families gathered together, all was silent, it was as if the whole country had downed tools and stopped silently for their return. Then, in the distance, two shining lights came into view, the lights from either side of the plane lit the path ahead but there was still silence and we saw the lights before we heard the engines, it was eerie and sad. I imagined Simon in that vast cavity of the plane and I held myself together but all I wanted to do was cry aloud for him. It was a magnificent craft, it was so silent, so graceful for such a large cumber sum plane, it flew past above our heads as it was to circle Wootton Bassett before its final decent to us. We didn't see it land as we went back inside whilst it did. Although we watched it on a monitor inside and waited until the preparations were finalized outside.

After it landed we were again escorted outside, where we sat under a shelter, a red carpet was respectively laid, it made a path towards the grey plane which stood silently, it's engines cut The back door slowly, quietly opened and from a distance, a Padre gave out prayers, his words echoing round the large airfield made it all the more moving. The sounds of sobbing interrupted the deadly silence as the first of four coffins were slowly carried from the back of the plane. I felt for every single family member as the sobbing intensified, slowly and surefooted, the Soldier Pall Bearers made their way to the back of a waiting hearse and some fought to hold their tears in. Simon was third in the row and as soon as I saw his coffin appear from the carrier, my legs nearly gave way. He was in there and in my mind I talked to him "I'm here Simon", I felt burning inside of me, I felt his presence now, it was so strong, I had not felt it so much when he was so far away but I did now and it intensified, that bond with Simon still there. As he passed us, draped in our Country's flag, I quietly wept, I wanted to hold him so bad, I felt for Pete as that was his boy in there. "I love you", I silently whispered and I watched him as his hearse disappeared from view. He's where he belongs, home.

An hour later we were on our way to the morgue. Simon and his friends were placed there for the families to visit. As we entered, the sealed coffin Simon now lay in was probably one of the ones he told me about, back in

March, when he got ready for his departure to Afghanistan. Whilst on the airstrip waiting to board the plane, he had seen empty coffins being loaded on and I was upset when he told me this. How presumptuous they were, I told him and he probably saw the same coffin that he was to own just five months later. As I entered the small room which held our son's flag covered coffin, I stopped, I backed up quickly, I couldn't look at that box, this wasn't how he should be coming home. I sat outside and this time grief got the better of me and I cried. Pete, Natalie and Stuart talked to him but I couldn't, I heard his voice from only weeks before "Hello mother" I felt I was letting him down. Pete came out and they said their goodbyes, I said it in my mind "Bye Simon, love you". We then left this place and met Simon's two young Escorts and thanked them for looking after our son, for two so young they did their job well and with respect.

We chose not to go into Wootton Bassett as it was too much to take in, the press was there in large numbers but this beautiful little town did our boys proud. They stood and saluted four young Heroes, these boys who had sacrificed their lives for their Country. The people who lined the road didn't know Simon, but they took time to show their respects to all the fallen Soldiers. We went back to the Hotel before the long journey home; we were to meet with the Coroner who was to look after Simon until he was returned back to us, in Cadishead, our home town. We were led into a large conference room where the Coroner, along with Army Personnel, chatted to each family individually. Our turn finally came, she introduced herself and offered condolences and we were told it would be a week before Simon came home. We asked "why so long?" "There are formalities that need to be dealt with first" she told us. "What formalities?" we enquired, and then the words that cut my heart into two were mentioned, "Post Mortem". "No we won't allow it" I cried, because he'd suffered enough but the Coroner spoke softly and said "we must". Even if we refused, this barbaric act was to take place anyway, poor Simon, I couldn't bear much more. "Why?" I asked, surely the cause of death was obvious but his bloody nightmare keeps going on and on and I dispelled the images from my mind.

Within the hour we were finally on our way home, numb, confused and missing Simon so much. That night after Major Mike had left us, Pete told Natalie and I, why there was a need for the Post Mortem. He was going to withhold the truth from us but he knew that we would uncover the reason why eventually and thought the right thing to do was to be honest with us. Simon had stepped on that savage I.E.D, his injuries were horrific and they needed to be certain as to the cause of death, hence the need for the Post Mortem. I'm not going into the extent of his injuries that is something that will remain unspoken and unwritten. The only thing on my mind is "did he suffer?" To know the answer to this question would ease my pain and if it was the answer I yearned to hear, it would comfort me some. We arrived home, strained and tired, hundreds of sympathy cards waited to be opened and I struggled to find a place for them all.

Repatriation

Simon's final resting place

The day after our return, Major Mike came by and the hard task to arrange the funeral was to begin. Simon was to have a Full Military Funeral, he had earned this and that's what he would have wanted. The date was set for Thursday 3rd September and in the meantime, life was on hold. The wait for Simon to come home to Cadishead was painful, the thought of burying him repeated in my mind, it was still unreal, we still couldn't sleep and we lived on takeaways as I couldn't be bothered to cook, as it didn't interest me. We were not particularly bothered if we ate or not, but we did, because we had Natalie. Each day passed, no difference, still that empty feeling, still counting heads. Major Mike brought us a framed photograph of Simon which had been taken just before he set of for Afghan, it was set in a crude handmade wooden frame and it was the same picture that stood on a table in Afghanistan during the memorial so we will never replace this frame.

The 100 mm Artillery Shell, along with a Cross constructed from shells from the 50 mm canon which was fired in Afghanistan, in salute to Simon, were both engraved with his name and Army number. They are very special to our family and they sit next to Simon's cabinet which holds all our precious items of his, including hackle, belts, medals and flags also the special Bible that kept my son occupied on those nights in Afghanistan. All this memorabilia will one day be passed down through the Annis family, never to be let go of, never to be sold, it will be stated in mine and Pete's Will that it all must be kept together or placed in a war museum, to be cared for, hopefully, for hundreds of years to come.

Pete's most treasured item is a brass Zippo lighter that Simon had bought for him one Christmas. It was with engraved on the side with the words *"Thanks for everything dad"*. These words are worn down now but the lighter stands in pride of place in his cabinet, as Pete is too scared to use it in case it gets lost. The Beret, on another shelf, is the one he had worn and I can smell Simon on this, I hold it to my heart sometimes and sniff into it deeply. I look at this cabinet each day and I wonder, "Will it get easier?" will I look at his things one day without the hurt it gives me. But I don't want it to get easier, because when it does, it will mean we are finally getting on with our lives and I don't want that stage to begin, personally I will not allow it.

We were informed that Simon was about to leave, to set off on his final journey home to Cadishead. They had released him into the care of our local Undertaker. He had undergone that examination, that word I don't want to say and now he was to come home to the town where he was born and bred, his familiar happy place. The following day, the Undertaker paid us a visit. Danny is a professional in his job and we knew Simon was in the best hands, he was a veteran in his line of work and we were completely happy leaving him with Danny. He was to clear out a large room for Simon so we could all sit together at ease, rather than squeezing into a small uncomfortable area and we were grateful to him. Simon arrived back to Cadishead but it was too late to visit so we would wait until the morning. That night it was hard for us to settle as Simon was home now, alone, waiting our visit.

The next morning slowly arrived and we were to go at 11am. We had photographs for him and were to take a pin board with us to put all the pictures on. There were baby photos, family photos but why we felt the need to do this, I'm not sure. We also made it very clear that no one was to come and see Simon. I know that Simon would agree with this decision as I needed people to remember him as he was, smiling and rapping with his songs. We went to visit our son, to see his beautiful young face. I had thought long and hard, "Would I go in that room where he lay, did I want to see him?" but I would't make a decision until the day came. Pete was to enter first, and then he would come and get me. Ten years previously, I had seen firstly Pete's father, who had sadly passed away in 1999, then my brother, later in the same year and I regretted seeing them both. The images I now see are not the ones that I'd like to remember and I didn't want this of Simon. I needed to see his face in his happy days and I know that he is my son but I know him well and he would not want me in there.

When we got there we were greeted by the Undertakers employee, Kath. The building was cold and although it was pleasantly decorated, I'm afraid that no tones of peach and red could warm the place up. Simon was in the second door, he now lay in an open casket, it was the best and the Army had spared no expense. He had on his full uniform, his Blues, his shiny boots, white gloves, and the uniform that was all too familiar to us in his proudest days. As discussed, Pete was to enter first, he told me he wanted to see his boy, but when he and Stuart walked reluctantly in, they immediately turned around and quickly left. I needed to remember my son's face as he was, larger than life, laughing, raising that cheeky eyebrow.

As Pete hurried out of Simon's room, I met his tearful eyes and he slowly shook his head. That's all I needed, no questions, I feel for Pete now, does that image of Simon haunt his memories now or does the happy living face of Simon overshadow them. I felt that I had let Simon down, he needed me but I couldn't do it, I couldn't go in there but I wanted him so badly, I wanted to squeeze him and ruffle his hair. I wanted to talk to him and whisper my private goodbyes but I think now that Simon would have understood. I found a chair and placed it just outside his door, not too far, but not too close that I could catch a glimpse. This was killing me but I resisted the urge to run in, pick him up and give his head a huge kiss. So for the first few days my place was outside away from my poor son, along with Pete, Natalie and Stuart. The worst time was when the quiet of night came, I missed him so much, he wasn't far from us, I felt him calling me. He was all alone in the cold Undertaker's parlor; he should have been home here, where he belonged.

I had a constant worry I needed to talk to Simon's Padre. He came on request and I told him my worries, that Simon hadn't been christened. We just didn't get round to it when he was a baby and when he was older, he didn't want it. I cried when I told the Padre this and I begged him to have Simon Christened. I am not really religious but I wanted everything to be right, "could he still enter heaven if he wasn't christened?" For this to play on my mind, I suppose I must believe in something or maybe I was in denial? He told us that Simon couldn't have this ritual, I was inconsolable but he calmed me down and told me that he could have a blessing instead. It comforted me when he said that this was like a Christening and so we agreed to it and it would take place the next day.

We met the Padre at the Undertakers the next day, he was dressed in all his regalia and I took my seat outside the door way of Simons room it was wide open, but I remained out of view. I felt bad, I wanted to sit with Simon during this important ritual and I hated myself for this. I think that Pete thought the same but it was too much for me to bear, to see him like this. The Padre began and we listened intently to every word he spoke, it was very moving. I knew when he had marked the sign of the Cross onto Simon's forehead as I felt it, but again I resisted the urge to go to my son. We sat and cried, silently we wept for him with Natalie by my side, pale and tearful. The Padre finished his sermon; "Amen" we repeated this quietly. I was comforted and relieved that this blessing had taken place, if heaven did truly exist, I now knew Simon had ticked all the right boxes to enter, although I didn't doubt that he would be allowed a place in God's Great Temple, weren't all hero's welcome? The next day we went back and gave Kath all our heartfelt letters which we had written to Simon, all our goodbyes and final words of love. These were to be placed in with Simon, along with photos, gifts and the watch Pete gave to him, he wore this always. They were placed inside his beautiful ornate coffin and then the lid was sealed forever. Now I could go to Simon and talk to him. I felt the side of the coffin where I thought his hand lay I touched this as I yearned to feel close to him. I stroked the top where I knew his head lay on his soft pillow, as close to him as I could get, I hoped he felt my comforting touch and warmth as I soothed away his pain.

The funeral was confirmed for Thursday 3rd September, the day our son will be laid in his final resting place. I still held the thought that it wasn't Simon in that wooden tomb, he was lost in Afghanistan, they would find him soon, and he would come back to us. The cemetery we had chosen was close to our home, just 15 minutes' walk away or five minutes in the car. How many times before had I passed this place when I picked Simon up from the Junior School in this small quiet village, how many times had I driven past it with the children in the back of the car, not once acknowledging it, why should I as we didn't know anyone in there. This cosy little cemetery in a Cheshire village called Hollins Green is small and peaceful, with trees and farm fields, with long crops of golden wheat swaying in the breeze, outlining its perimeter, making it all the less stressful. Squirrels busily run around the headstones, truly a fitting place for a Hero to take his long earned rest.

The week running up to the funeral was busy, sad and very stressful as everything needed to be perfect. People asked if we wanted flowers or donations and I replied that we wanted flowers by the hundreds for him. Two beautiful songs were chosen, the first was "Heaven" by DJ Sammy and the second was "Footprints" by Leona Lewis. The verse "Footprints in the Sand "is very precious to us as Simon carried it on a little laminate card inside his wallet and we only read it after his death, it obviously meant something to him. Both songs were sad and moving harmonies. Two hearses were ordered and an extra one was arranged to carry the many wreaths that were expected.

Many seats in the church had to be reserved and I had to venture out to buy a suitable dress, but Pete already had a suit to wear. A booklet was made with Simon's happy photos inside, showing him in his early years and later when he was attired in his Army uniforms. Although everything was finally organized for the day we would have much preferred a large glass carriage drawn by four large strong black horses, if we had been financially blessed, but sadly the black hearse had to take its place. We knew this was to be a day where possibly hundreds of locals would join us in paying respects to our boy. Cadishead and Irlam are small towns connected together and Simon is the first local Soldier to die in a war since world war two, so we have been told, but I am not sure if this is true or not. The local people of these two small towns hold special thoughts of Simon, he was their local Hero and I do genuinely believe that they cared about his fate. Being a small town people know each other whether by sight or name, Simon grew up here and the Annis families have a very large circle of friends, Simon was one of their own and we were willing to share our family grief with them.

The 3rd September was drawing closer and we visited Simon each day. I wanted him to remain here in this building; I didn't want him to go into the ground that was all too final. At least here he was only inches from me, the darkness and cold earth on top of him frightened me, I was frightened for him. We would still sit in the early hours, unable to sleep, trying to make sense of it all and I had the thought of Simon's death in my mind. This time last year, he had just celebrated his 21st Birthday, he was alive and well, in Belize. Who would have forecast what was to happen 12 months later? Our home was constantly busy but I knew that one day we would be left alone, I knew it would be then that the emptiness of our home and the realization of the past 4 weeks would hit us. I dreaded the future now, as our family of five was now down to a family of four. "Time" people told us, "give it time" but as far as I was concerned there could be endless time ahead of us and it still wouldn't be enough. The week dragged on, still eating takeaways, still counting heads, more news of lost Soldiers and I felt new grief over and over again for the distraught families. Pete and I received letters from mothers who also had lost their treasured sons. How strong they are and I hope that one day I will find the strength to write to a grieving mother, only time will tell. Dealing with grief isn't something we can be taught, it isn't set in stone as to what path we must follow to endure this terrible part of our life, it's a lonely thing.

On the eve of Simon's funeral, we went along to visit him at the Undertaker's for the last time; his coffin was now draped in the flag of our Country, my baby boy, memories flashed through my mind. I thought of him as a baby sitting in his chair, playing contentedly with his wooden spoons, chatting happily to himself and then I remembered something long forgotten. As a toddler, Simon would be propped up on Pete's knee. Pete had a song that Simon loved and he used to sing it to him, I can hear his cute giggle now, that contagious cute giggle, the song went like this:-

This is the song for tiny little people,
Tiny little people, to sing
You see these, these are my knees,
You see those, those are my toes.

As he was singing, Pete would squeeze Simon's knees, the next line was his toes but before Pete got to them, Simon would begin giggling uncontrollably in anticipation of tickling toes. *"Poor Simon"* I whispered *"you had so much to do, so much to live for"* as tears again rolled down my face, how the hell can I live with so much pain? That night we had to leave Simon, "your big day tomorrow, sleep tight mummies little Soldier" I whispered while I gave his hair one last imaginary ruffle through the lid of his wooden tomb. We left the Undertaker's for the last time. That night dragged and we stayed up and sat silently in the dark of the home, preparing ourselves for what was to come.

The church was to be full, all seats at the front were now reserved, we couldn't accommodate everyone and some people were not happy. This made me very angry, did it matter where they sat, wasn't it enough that they were there, the day was for Simon, to remember him, not about who got front seat or not. Apart from the last minute hitches, all was set and speakers had been put up outside the church for the expectant masses of people who would be unable to get in, the many hundreds who would help us through this day.

The morning of the 3rd was now upon us, we had to ready ourselves, for the day was here and we had to bury our son, more flowers were delivered and we were overwhelmed by the masses of beautiful wreaths that had been sent, some from people we didn't know. The day was bright and dry but the strong gale force wind made everything so noisy. My stomach was churning, I felt sick and light headed, our nerves were shot, and the shaking of mine and Pete's hands gave this away. We hadn't done this before, there was no rehearsal but we were comforted by Major Mike who was there to watch over us. We left the house, locked the door and we all stood in the front garden, the wind so forceful, the roar it made was making it difficult to hear spoken words. Simon was now on his way, he was coming home to his happy place, his childhood place. The hearse carried him through the streets of Cadishead, slowly it made its way towards us, to his Mum, Dad, Stuart and Natalie. As we stood waiting for him there was an eerie presence, although the wind spoilt the silence, the normally busy street now empty, people avoided it this day. Then we saw Simon, he was just turning the corner, before the long stretch of road to his home, the hearse slowly and silently crept towards us and as I spotted him an overwhelming sense of loss hit me. "*Simon*" I cried, our son had finally come home, but in a way we could not have imagined.

Opposite our home, there's a Junior School and the older children were now outside, they lined the street, very maturely they stood, 10yr olds all showing respect to a man they didn't know, I felt proud they were there for Simon. The hearse came to a halt, the many flowers were placed into the second car, our wreath of an angel was placed next to the framed photo of Simon, his face looked out of the back window for all to see, even a wreath from his much loved pet Mojo was placed beside him. We slowly took our seats, I looked at Simon's photo that faced us from the car in front and I smiled at him. We started the slow haunting journey to the church which was over a mile away, another day to overcome, another hurdle to cross.
A community normally buzzing with town life, stood still as if time itself had stood still, sad faces filled the pavements, heads bowed, silently, Simon passed each and every one of them, the silence broken by sobs.

People sobbed for a Hero, they sobbed for the loss of a boy too young to bear the burden of war on his innocent shoulders, strangers sobbed for this sacrifice, all to ensure a better and safer life for them. But most of all they sobbed because they knew Simon and all the town sobbed because he was their local boy, it was all too close to home for them as for most, the reality of this bloody brutal war was now a reality and all too plain to see. They held red roses in their hands, a gift for Simon. The slow quiet drone of the black hearse being the only noise, as it idled slowly through the streets, the same streets that Simon himself had walked down so many times. I couldn't look through the windows, I couldn't look people in the eyes, their hurt, hurt me and I felt sorrow from the many hundreds of people. I wanted to carry their sadness in my heart, I wanted to feel sadness and sorrow. I didn't deserve happiness now that Simon had lost the chance to experience it ever again.

We couldn't believe what we were seeing as hundreds of people now lined the path to our destination. Police and Fire Brigade personnel, in full uniform, all saluted our son as he passed them by, all heads lowered in silent prayer. Roses covered Simon's hearse and the pride I had for my son intensified. I told him "see Dobber, people do care", they are grateful. Simon wasn't just another statistic, he was someone, he was special, I knew that then and I knew what I had to do. I would endeavor to keep his memory alive. As we approached the large church, the crowd intensified.

'The Service'

Hundreds of mourners gathered to pay tribute to our son, Fusilier Simon Annis, who died as he tried to save his commander. As the crowd of mourners, including active and former servicemen and women, stretched out of the church grounds, the booklet containing photos of Simon in his baby years as well as Army years were handed out. His coffin, carried by fellow Soldiers, was draped in the Union Flag and adorned with a wreath of poppies. Ten other members from his Regiment formed a Guard of Honor, as ex-servicemen lowered the Standards in tribute. We were met at the entrance by the Reverend, then the song we had chosen rang out. There were words of welcome and prayer, and then the hymn," Oh God our help in ages past"was then sung. After more prayers, the second hymn, "Onward Christian Soldiers" was also sung. The memories that were read out were a fitting tribute to Simon, the first was by Stuart who said. "Simon has made me the proudest brother in the world and to continue to live without my ray of sunshine seems impossible. However, I stand with pride as I am the brother of a true Hero". Then Mattie rose to his feet, I previously doubted if he would go through with it but he kept himself together and with a shaky, tearful voice said "I am very proud to have known Simon and will never forget him". Then Simon's good friend Sgt John Royle read a prayer. The Chaplains address by Padre Jerry was read out.

The Fuller Exhortation -

They went with songs to the battle
They were young, straight of limb
True of eye, steady and aglow

They were staunch to the end
Against odds uncounted they fell
With their faces set towards the foe.

Remembrance:-

They shall not grow old as we that are left grow old,
Age shall not weary them, nor the years condemn
At the going down of the sun, and in the morning.......
We will remember them!

As the last post was offered, all flags, standards and colours were lowered. Silence for one minute followed and as the Bugler played, I saw images of Simon running scared to his friend. After the Reveille, the Lord's Prayer was softly spoken by all present. Then, the Army Padre, Jerry Sutton, who led the service with the Reverend David Wheeler said

"The Soldier's irresistible cheekiness and inherent joy brought a smile to so many people; he was able to make the best of things, however hard they might be"

As we rose, we followed Simon towards the entrance as the song "Heaven" filled the air, mourners stood silently as his coffin was carried from the church. We took our seats in the waiting vehicle and as we left the church behind, there was a mass applause as the cortège moved away. Now Simon had started his journey to his final resting place. People still lined the streets but this time instead of silence they applauded him as he passed them by. As Police motorbikes sped up and down ensuring an easy unbroken route, I didn't want to think about what awaited us, it seemed all so final.

As we approached the small village of Hollins Green, scores of cars were following behind us. On arrival at the cemetery, we stopped in front of the large iron rustic gates, the wind now swirling violently as the bearers of the Standards battled hard to hold them straight. The Pall Bearers took their place and lifted Simon's coffin onto their shoulders, the final walk to the prepared grave was long and slow. We followed behind, still numb and as we stood at this place we had to wait a few minutes for the crowd to catch up, many finding it hard to find a parking spot. The cemetery filled and as there wasn't enough room for all, so many waited outside the gates. Just to be present was enough for them. Simon was immensely proud of the job he did and a military funeral would be his wishes had we given him the option. The plot had been bought by the M.O.D and they own this now, so the head stone, which is to be placed with Simon, will be permanently looked after and we have comfort in this knowledge. He will be forever cared for, long after we have left this earth. We stood close together, prayers were given, the wind whistling around the small cemetery made it difficult to stand firm. Simon was gently, slowly guided down into this deep dark hole, I cried for him, "poor Simon", if he was looking down on us now, what were his thoughts. "Bye, bye sweetheart" I spoke to him in my mind. I was then offered earth; I walked over to him and let this drop onto him. Pete did the same, a father so proud of his boy and he wept so much for him. As family members took their turn in this role, more prayers were given.

Then the gun salute ripped through the silence, respect to a fallen Soldier. Somewhere in the distance a Bugler started to sound the "Last Post", this sombre music echoed around the silent cemetery. We would hear this so often after Simon's death, it always brings a tear to my eye. We have recently found out that the Last Post has words attached to it and after more investigation we have found the alleged origin to this sad heartfelt tune. Below is what I was sent by a friend:-

Butterflies and Feathers

The Last Post

If you have ever been to a military funeral in which the last post was played: this will bring a new meaning to it. Here is something everyone should know. Until I read this, I didn't know, but I checked it out and it's true. We have all heard the haunting song, 'The Last Post.' it's the song that gives us the lump in our throats and usually tears in our eyes. But, do you know the story behind the song? If not, I think you will be interested to find out about its humble beginnings.

Reportedly, it all began in 1862 during the American civil war, when union Army Captain Robert Ellicombe was with his men near Harrisons landing in Virginia. The Confederate Army was on the other side of the narrow strip of land.

During the night, Captain Ellicombe heard the moans of a soldier who lay severely wounded on the field. Not knowing if it was a union or confederate soldier, the Captain decided to risk his life and bring the stricken man back for medical attention, crawling on his stomach through the gun fire, the Captain reached the stricken soldier and began pulling him towards his encampment.

When the Captain finally reached his own lines, he discovered it was actually a confederate soldier, but the soldier was dead.

The Captain lit a lantern and suddenly caught his breath and went numb with shock, in the dim light, he saw the face of the soldier, it was his own son. The boy had been studying music in the south when the war broke out. Without telling his father, the boy enlisted in the confederate army.

The following morning, heartbroken, the father asked permission of his superiors to give his son a full military burial, despite his enemy status. His request was only partially granted.

The Captain had asked if he could have a group of army band members play a funeral dirge for his son at the funeral. The request was turned down since the soldier was a confederate.

But, out of respect for the father, they did say they could give him only one musician.

The Captain chose a bugler. He asked the bugler to play a series of musical notes he had found on a piece of paper in the pocket of the dead youths uniform. This wish was granted. The melody, we now know as 'The Last Post' used at military funerals was born.

The service for Simon's interment was over. The many hundreds of mourners filed passed us, offering condolences, their faces just a blur, I couldn't take much in and I wanted to be left alone to sit with Simon. Our duty of care for Simon started from birth, nappy changes, and playtimes, educating him in ways of life, clothing him and keeping him safe. Then he grew into a man, only then did we renounce our duties for him and his independence took over. Now he has come back to us, our duties for the care of him begin again. A mother and father's role never go away, no matter how old their child is, in life and in death.

We were swept away, the wake awaited us. It was held at the Royal Arms Club, chosen because of its large hall, on arrival, food and much needed hot drinks were on offer and over 500 people came back to the hall with us. We bought two large leather bound remembrance books, these were laid out on the top table along with his flag and medals, his large picture took centre stage and people queued patiently to write their heartfelt messages to a Soldier some didn't know.

The room was full to the brim, so many faces, we felt the need to thank each person personally, we were so thankful for their attendance and I was completely overwhelmed by the turn out. The Fusilier's toast drink is port, so we bought bottles, how many I am not sure of, we filled small shot glasses and offered these to the large crowd. Major Mike then stood up and announced the toast, he said *"For Simon, once a Fusilier always a Fusilier"* everyone then toasted our son. How do people cope with grief, for me obviously it's a life sentence, but later on that night, I grew bitter when my 36 year old nephew told me something that had happened. Outside the hall, some Soldiers, along with someone who Simon thought of very dearly, were acting rowdily, and loudly laughing and one person was actually performing handstands, although the small black dress she was wearing didn't do enough to cover her up. Then to top it all, these certain individuals thought it was a good idea to finish the night off by going clubbing. Did they think they had just attended a wedding or a birthday; sadly Simon wasn't important enough to sadden their day.

One day they might just realize that losing someone so close to them isn't an excuse to party. I put all this to the back of my mind and as long as Simon had his true family to remember and cherish his memory, did it matter what some soulless people did. It was now late but we felt we had to stay until the last person had finally left which eventually they did. Now in this large empty hall, quiet now, I stood with Pete and Natalie, "this is it", I thought "it's all over". We quietly gathered Simon's precious items together and left. The short five minute walk home felt like miles as we didn't speak. We entered our home, it was dark and quiet "what do we do now?" I asked Pete, he looked at me with damp eyes "I don't know" he said. After 3 frantic weeks we were alone, we hadn't had time to think, it had all been so chaotic, that night the three of us started to grieve for Dobber. Sleep didn't happen and I heard Natalie at 4am, we couldn't settle.

The next day came, 4th September 2009. We found it hard to sit and do nothing, we had to keep ourselves busy and that's the way it's been ever since. We started to plan the Sponsored Walk in aid of the Fusilier Society, for the "*Simon Annis Appeal*". It would be a 15 mile walk and would take a massive amount of organising but we would do it. So that was it and from 5th September the ball was rolling. We started to organise fund raising events. Life sadly has to go on but we were not coping, we couldn't say Simon's name, we kept our grief to ourselves, we all cried but only when we were alone, life was impossible but we kept ourselves active.

After only six weeks, we all had to go back to work as the mortgage and direct debits didn't pay themselves. It was too early to return to work and I knew it didn't help but it felt that we had to get back to normal. Ok, Simon is buried and life should be back to normal now, but no, it wasn't right. The longer time went on, the more we missed him, it was horrendous. Pete had to return to work, whether he wanted to or not as he is the main earner. Natalie also had to, as we just couldn't support her. I too went back and I tried so hard but in the restaurant where I worked a large flat screen TV adorned the wall and it was set to Sky News. I could be serving customers whilst a broadcast from Wooten Basset was on, showing another repatriation and I would then disappear outside to cry alone.

Sadly, only two weeks after I started back at work, I walked out during the dinner time rush. I quietly walked to the lockers, got my coat and walked away from my job. I cried all the way home, I couldn't take any more.

Major Mike organised a Counselor for me, she made an appointment and came to my home, she explained that the grieving process comes in stages and I was at one of these stages. I was angry, I didn't want to see people, I could walk around Tesco and I ignored people I knew, I resented them all for having a complete family. I had one visit off her, I didn't want anymore, I think looking back now that I wanted to feel this bad because if she made me feel better, it would mean I was eventually accepting my grief and I didn't want this, I still don't. I felt so guilty, I had no job and Pete had to support us both, it hurt me so much to see him persevere.

One day Major Mike came by, we had to decide what was to be put on Simon's head stone, this wasn't a hard decision although nothing of a personal nature could be added. We chose the right one for him, the top of the cream coloured stone was to have the Fusilier emblem cut into it and in the middle of this distinctive emblem it has the words:

"HONI.SOIT.QUI.MAL.Y.PENSE."

This is the Motto of the Royal Regiment of Fusiliers and when translated means; "Evil be to him who evil thinks". At the bottom of Simon's head stone is a Latin quote:

"ARTE ET MARTE"

This means *"By skill by fighting"* and then came the words we requested, *"The day you left, a little bit of us went with you"*. His head stone would not be ready until February 2010 so in the meantime, Danny, our good friend the Undertaker, had a Pine Cross made for us, with a brass plaque bearing Simon's name and age. This was a lovely gesture and we were very grateful, but shortly after the fitting of the cross, I received a phone call informing us that no temporary crosses were allowed and if we wanted it to remain we would have to pay a fee. After a phone call, the Council backed down. I would have sat on Simon's grave, day and night, to ensure that our son's plot didn't go unmarked, even for a short time.

I was livid, but all this was soon settled. In the meantime we tended to Simon every single day. I remember last October 2009, the winds again visited us and as we walked to see him, we saw that his plot was covered in leaves, autumn had finally arrived. He must have been laughing at us as we frantically tried to clear all the fallen leaves off him and as we did this another gust brought more down on him. It was a tedious waste of time but I wanted him to look perfect. When his plot started the natural process of sinking, we bought large heavy bags of top soil and emptied them onto the grave until it reached the same level of his neighbors. Then we planted over 300 spring bulbs so that next year he is going to look amazing.

Eventually when his head stone was ready to be set in place, we took the pine cross home and it now sits in the garden where Simon happily and contentedly played with his ants. We visit Simon each and every day and have bought a small push along lawn mower so that we can cut his grass twice a week. The Council does this, but we much prefer to do it ourselves. His flowers are never allowed to wilt, we top them up once a week and sometimes if the weather is bad we change them twice.

The boot of our car isn't used for storing shopping now as it's full of watering cans, clippers, sweeping brush and the lawn mower. There is a large old lime tree that grows tall, opposite to Simon and there's a large thick branch that splits off into two parts. I have always imagined my son perched on this branch, looking down on us, right from the day of the funeral my eyes were drawn to this spot. I see him with his knees drawn up and his hands clutching them tightly to him. I always smile at him up there, no one saw me do this as it was mine and Simon's secret.

Simon's favorite verse which he carried in his wallet was "Footprints in the Sand". So special it was to him and I would like to share it with you:-

Ann Annis

Footprints in the sand

*One night I dreamed I was walking along the beach with the Lord.
Many scenes from my life flashed across the sky.
In each scene I noticed footprints in the sand.
Sometimes there were two sets of footprints.
Other times there were one set of footprints.*

*This bothered me because I noticed that during the low periods of my life,
When I was suffering from anguish, sorrow or defeat,
I could see only one set of footprints.*

*So I said to the lord,
"You promised me lord that if I followed you, you would walk with me always.
But I have noticed that during the most trying periods of my life
There have only been one set of footprints in the sand.
Why, when I needed you most, you have not been there for me?"*

*The Lord replied "The times you have seen only one set of footprints in the sand,
Is when I carried you"*

Butterflies and Feathers

Simons funeral and final resting place

Simmons Name on the Arboretum

Ann Annis

Butterflies and feathers

I am skeptical towards the beliefs and stories of the afterlife although it would be easier for me to accept such things. Maybe there is truth behind stories and tales of ghosts and strange occurrences within the home. I sometimes think we look for things that are not truly there because we want to believe, it gives us connections to those who are lost to us.

Five days after our Simon died; I thought that I sensed him around me he talked to me in my mind. After his internment in that dark cold resting place, I had thoughts in my mind that he waited each day for us to visit and tend his plot. We go to see him daily as we feel guilty if we don't, we don't want to let him down. Unaccountable things did happen in the home the radio upstairs had the habit of switching itself on, it happened a lot but only for three days. The large heavy ornamental clock on the mantel lifted and rested against the wall, again no explanation but I'm still very skeptical.

Imagine tiny fluffy feathers, they float down wherever we step, they block my path, they appear in abundance, everywhere, shortly after Simon died and as I have said, I do not really believe but I am making myself believe. In the home, when we sit, a feather floats from nowhere. Once, I was sitting in the middle of a crowded beach, there was no wind, just a rare hot sunny day and I was writing when it came down and rested on my knee. I sit in our conservatory with no drought to alter its path, when this one fell to the floor at my feet. Pete and I began to notice them and if they wanted our attention, they had it. It happened every time we spoke of Simon, they came clean and immaculate. Each time I see a feather now, I pick it up and stroke it, I smile and say "thanks Dobber"I told Pete "Simon has his wings now, he's an angel and when he talks to us, he gently plucks away one of his feathers and blows it down to us" We laugh together, saying he must be nearly bald by now.

At the same time, butterflies in all their beauty descended on us. It started one day as Pete and I were sat with friends outside, enjoying the sunshine. A large white butterfly came to me, although we were amongst a crowd it hovered above my head and I gently wafted it away but it persevered. The crowd now silent watched the beautiful sight as this delicate creature circled relentlessly. I then stretched out my arm and spread my fingers as the creature slowly came to rest on my finger tip. It rested there for only seconds then it took flight and came to rest on my closed lips, where it sat a while before lifting off. It then flew upwards and out of sight. "Simon's just kissed me"I said as a tear flowed down my cheek. The next day it was to be Pete's turn to encounter another of these delicate creatures.

A large red butterfly circled his head as he was about to come through the door, he tried to waft it away but it showed no fear as it persevered tapping Pete's head, as in attack. It wanted to come into the house and it was doing its best, it was frantic with its quest. Pete blocked the doorway and eventually it gave up and made its way upwards out of sight. This happened only twice, once to Pete and once to me and we haven't encountered anything like this since but the little pure white feathers still like to make an appearance every now and then.

We have a nephew, he's only four years old, small, cute and likes lots of hugs and kisses, Simon was very fond of this little lad, and his name is Asa. Now what happened with Asa puzzles me and makes me wonder if there is anything real about the talk of spiritualism, I only wish I knew for certain. Many months after Simon died, Asa went along with his mum and dad to the local Burger King for a treat, and they left him in the car in the car park with his brother, while they collected their food. Upon returning to the car, they seated themselves and started to drive away. Vicky, his mum, asked Asa if he was ok, he replied "I've just blown Simon a kiss" and with this, Vicky told her partner Alan to stop the car, as normally Asa only blew Simon a kiss when he was with her or at Simon's grave. Vicky then asked "why did you blow Simon a kiss" and Asa pointed to a spot in the car park at shoulder height, not up in the sky and he told her "because Simon was over there".

Innocently he said "he had a dinosaur under his arm, not a real one mummy, a toy one". Vicky took this statement in her stride, although Asa wasn't one to make up imaginative stories. It was only when I was told this, that the shock on their faces told a story. I told them Simon indeed had owned a toy dinosaur when he was very small, as mentioned in this book earlier, it was one of his favourites and just being a toy, it wasn't a conversation piece. Asa had no way of knowing this; the lad could have said it was a teddy or a toy car that Simon was holding.

This story did however upset me immensely. Did it mean Simon was unhappy and craving for the life he could no longer have. However, a week later I was told that a "Medium" had sent a message and I felt comforted when she told me "Simon's not unhappy, this sighting means he has gone back to the happiest times in his past life". Again, do I believe? What will it take? I don't know for sure but maybe if my son had personally visited me then maybe I would find comfort in knowing he's in a far better place.

November 2009

Remembrance Day was fast approaching and Pete and I were torn between attending the local parade or the large event in Manchester. We were invited to attend the Manchester one but after this year we would commit ourselves to the local parade forever after. Over the years we have supported this event but this year it was to be a moving, upsetting reminder for us as our son was to be remembered along with the many thousands who had sadly lost their lives in all the wars, past and present and we were now part of a large family of those who are in the same sad situation as us.

We laid our wreath of poppies in recognition for all their bravery and loyalty to their Country, life had changed now for us, we felt we had to do more and more. We were inundated with invitations to various functions and it got out of hand. At one point it made me feel ill, I felt suffocated, I didn't feel like myself any more. On a trip to the doctor, she told me I had taken on too much and I needed to slow down and allow myself time to grieve. It was only when I did this, would I take in and accept that Simon had truly gone. I was still in denial, I still felt it was all a mistake and mistaken identity still entered my thoughts. We did slow down but it only made things worse, we had too much time on our hands which only gave us more time for thought, so we got back into a life of fundraising.

The sending of parcels to our troops became a large part of what we were doing and Pete's sister, Lynne who was an angel herself, managed all this for us, regardless of the TV reports that said the Troops were getting enough. It was reported that they were getting everything they needed but I knew that this was rubbish as my son had relied on these precious gifts from home He wasn't in Camp Bastion but was stationed in a Forward Operating Base (F.O.B) and he had relied on these. What harm could sending the parcels do? Was it just too expensive to get them out there or was transport a problem, I am not sure but the Annis parcels were still going.

Lynne does a fantastic job although she works full time, she carries on relentlessly and in each parcel she encloses a small laminate photograph of her precious nephew. She has sent out hundreds of parcels now and will continue to do so until the happy day comes, when all our boys are back home safe and well. The letters of thanks from the receivers of these parcels are a great inspiration for her, the lads are so grateful and some of them bring tears to our eyes when they express how grateful they were to get one of the parcels, just when they needed them. Some write and tell her they don't receive any from home and then I remember how I used to worry about Simon, imagining he got none whilst his mates opened theirs. To this day parcels are still being sent.

Simons Sponsored Walk

It's now nearing the walk which has taken three long hard months to put together as everything ad to be right and it meant that the many family meetings went on late into the night. We had to organize such a large event and it really did give us sleepless nights. Some people thought it was just a matter of turning up on the day but it was more than that. We had to meet with the local Police and keep them updated, we had to arrange liabilities cover, Stewards for the day and the Corp of Drummers had to be arranged. The Royal Arms Club was to supply food at the finish of the walk and over 1500 sheets had to be printed out. Sponsor Forms, Declarations, Gift Aid Forms all had to be signed on the day, it was done with military precision. It had to be otherwise it could have all turned disastrous.

We arrived early on the day to help with the erecting of the three tents which were needed. T-shirts were handed out with Simon's face digitally printed on the front and each person had to collect a minimum of £10 to cover the cost of these. The start of the walk was directly in front of the small village cemetery where our Dobber lay and as I saw his large lime tree from the road, I looked up and smiled at him. As people began to arrive, I realized it was going to be a great success and overall 500 people turned out and they all wore Simon's t-shirt. I was proud of them all. I took my place at the start line along with Pete, Natalie and Stuart and I was overwhelmed as I looked at the crowd, we didn't expect this.

The walk began and the paths were a sea of maroon coloured T-shirts, it was a day to remember. There wasn't any trouble, although we did have a few undesirable characters that shouldn't have been there but it made no difference, as nothing would spoil this day. At the half-way point we were met by the Drummers, who put on a show and the crowd loved them. On the way back the heavens opened, rain came down with such force that we were all saturated but no one cared. On the home stretch, the rain stopped and the most beautiful rainbow appeared. This made some people, along with myself, cry and the word got round that Simon had said "Thank You". It was a fitting end to a truly fabulous day, a lot of money was raised that day and the public support from our local area was second to none.

After all the hard work arranging the walk, we had one final fundraiser, a Xmas Disco. It was an amazing night and the turnout was fantastic, the support was there again. It was so busy and was standing room only by 8.30pm. A good start for an Annual Disco!

Christmas 2009

Now Xmas was here, the first without Simon. I used to adore Christmas; I was like a two year old. I started the preparations as early as September and now we dreaded it. After all the hard work throughout the year, we had peace and quiet for the first time. Again no tree was assembled, no tinsel and no Christmas lunch. Natalie went to stay with Nick's family over the festive period as to us it was now just another day. I know Simon wouldn't want this but we felt we were betraying him if we celebrated it because he also loved Christmas as much as we did. So many beautiful memories of Christmas's gone by, childhood laughter and play, favourite Christmas movies watched cosied up near the open fire, eating tins and tins of sweets. All this has gone now and it wouldn't be the same if we did try.

New Year's Eve, we went to the Coach and Horses again, this was a bad idea as the moment we sat amongst the happy party goers we missed our boy so much and I spent most of the night in the solitude of the toilet, crying for him. It was only the year before that Simon was with us, fighting with Mattie in the loo and coming out all red faced after a bout of wrestling with his best buddy. The chair he sat in the previous year was now filled by a stranger but each time I looked at this chair I saw Simon's worried face. We didn't celebrate the New Year. Will we again? Only time will tell.

Armed forces memorial 2010

A Service of Commemoration, to remember and give thanks for those who gave their lives in the service of their Country, was to be held at the National Memorial Arboretum on 5th June 2010. Another hurdle for us to climb. We have a constant reminder that Simon is dead as pre-booked events tell us that it's for our boy. We arrived in anticipation of what was to happen, we met the families of the other boys sadly lost to us. Large marquees were erected for the occasion, food and drink laid out for all.

His Royal Highness, The Earl of Wessex, along with other high dignitaries were to attend. The memorial was designed to provide fitting recognition for the British Servicemen and Women who have been killed on duty since the end of the Second World War but it is not a war memorial. Alongside the names of those killed in conflict are the names of those killed in peacekeeping missions such as Bosnia and Herzegovina, in training accidents or as a result of terrorist action. This day was to honour those who died on duty in 2009. When we took our places, the service was to begin, together were all the families united in grief. There were various readings and prayers and then the newly added names were read out. Although we are aware of what has happened and where Simon now lies, every time his name is read aloud, it's like a thunder bolt to our hearts, it still shocks us.

The Last Post rang out from a lone Bugler, followed by a two minute silence, the Reveille followed and then the final blessing, everyone then stood up to sing the National Anthem. We all then lined up and slowly made our way to lay down our wreaths and as we approached the place where Simon's name was carved into one of these great stones, the nerves in my stomach took over. As I turned the corner, my eyes met his name amongst his friends, it was carved in stone, "S Annis". I cried at the sight, another thunder bolt tore through me; our son's name was now amongst 16,000 others. *"Oh Simon"* I said as we lay down our wreath of poppies. How sad there are so many large plain and empty stone pillars, all waiting for a name. Would we go back one day and find that these bare pillars of stone have been filled with the names of more young brave Soldiers?

The Inquest

We are into the Summer of 2010, the year has passed by so quickly and that fateful day when we heard the words, which I recount over and over again, "have you a son in Afghanistan called Simon Annis" It only seems like weeks have gone by, life hasn't changed much, memories are still hurting and strong, we have bad days and we have ok days but we don't have normal days anymore. We still keep busy and visit our Dobber daily.

It is July 7th 2010 and we are now travelling the long journey to Wiltshire, to attend the inquest of our son. I still have the unanswered question that I need to ask, "Did he die instantly?" Today I may find the answer to this. Weeks before, we had received the incident report as to what happened on that horrific sad day. Pete had so many questions he needed answering but one in particular needed to be verified .As Simon helped pick up the stretcher that was used to evacuate James Fullerton, he trod on the deadly I.E.D that killed all three and injured two more. We were told that the ground around the scene had been swept during an "Op Barma" drill to locate these I.E.D's and that the area was clear but this wasn't so. Pete felt that Simon had fatally found one of the I.E.D's which had not been detected and we needed to hear the answer to this.

We arrived at the Court and took our seats along with the families of the other boys who were with Simon on that tragic day. As the proceedings began, it was made very clear that this Coroner's Court was not a Court of Law. That meant we couldn't cross examine the witnesses, we couldn't argue our case and we were there just to determine how and when they died.

Shortly after 0300 hours on Sunday 16th August 2009, Simon set off on foot patrol. He was responsible for operating the light machine gun and under cover of darkness he and his section moved out on foot towards the intended objective. It was clear but very dark as there was only a quarter moon. At around 0500 hours, a large explosion occurred; the Section Commander had apparently detonated a "Pressure plate activated Improvised Explosive Device"Simon was amongst several Soldiers who immediately provided emergency medical assistance to his Commander (James Fullarton), who Simon was extremely fond of. This must have been horrendous for him, to see his true pal in this situation.

We were told later how they had heard someone shouting Fully's (James Fullarton) name and I wonder now was this call from Simon, as he ran to help him. Simon then helped others put Fully onto the stretcher and then onwards to the designated helicopter landing site so that he could be evacuated from the scene, as it had been said that Op Barma drills had been carried out to clear the route. Simon took the front of the stretcher whilst Louis took the other corner, they had only advanced a few metres when a second explosion ripped through the night, and this was what ended the lives of Simon and his two friends.

In the reports, it said that after poor Fully had been hit, clouds of dust hung thick in the air, they said that Simon was clearly in shock. As he led Fully away, he was looking up at the sky; he had to be constantly reassured. When Simon trod on this murderous I.E.D, he was thrown 25 to 30 metres away. The area was littered with I.E.Ds and over nine more were found later. The question that I longed to hear the answer to remained unanswered. Simon was too far away, on his own, face down in the mud. They didn't realize where he was at first, so no one got to him immediately. Screaming was heard after the second explosion, but from who no one knows. Did Simon live for a while, did he scream out for help, no one knows. This will haunt me from now to the day I die and these are the dreams I now have that keep me up during the night. As for Pete's question, "Why didn't the Op Barma pick up on the I.E.D that was responsible for Simon's death? " Answers were given, but the other question is "Are the Op Barmas adequate enough for the important role they serve?" This question was put to the poor lad who operated the equipment. He was under pressure in front of the Court and with his Commanding Officer watching him sternly and after a long pause of uncertainty, the lad said "Yes, they were adequate". So that was it, no arguments, no cross examining of the witnesses and we came away with some questions still unanswered. It was a disturbing day and now it was over. Still, that question of mine remains unanswered.

Homecoming parade

On the 1st December 2009, Pete and I were invited to attend the home coming parade; we were to meet the mayor of Salford along with lieutenant colonel Glover. Residents were to line the streets for the homecoming of soldiers who have returned from Afghanistan. The 2nd battalion of the fusiliers will be marching to the civic centre in Swinton, we arrived and were greeted, anticipation of what was to happen brought a dread within us, this day we should have seen our son amongst these fine young men. We took our places on the platform, along with the colonel, major mike and many others; we heard the corp. of drummers as the parade neared us. Thousands of well-wishers now crowded the streets, waving small flags, applause rang out. Around 250 soldiers took part in the parade. As the parade marched proudly by us, they turned and saluted us, that's when it hit me, I found I was unknowingly looking for Simon, he would have loved this setting, he would have marched so proud, we applauded the soldiers for the job they had completed but our son wasn't amongst them and I found it difficult to be happy and joyous. But obviously we were very relieved that they were now home.

Letter from Gordon Brown

After Simon's death, we received many letters, hundreds came, mostly from strangers and we read them all. There were letters from Brigadiers, Colonels and one from the Secretary of State but when a letter from 10 Downing Street, off Gordon Brown, dropped onto the mat, I had mixed feelings about it. Even though there was a lot of controversy at the time, I decided to remain mutual on the subject until I had opened and read it.

When I opened it, I realized it was hand written and I know what had been said about these letters in the news reports, but I have my own opinion and it's nothing to do with politics. He could easily have had this letter typed on behalf of himself, with only a signature required, but his own hand had written this.

It was scribbly and unreadable in parts but for me it was personal and he and his wife had shown true support and offered us their condolences. I understand that his eyesight is not too good but he had hand written this to make it more special. I am not concerned as to whether he did it as part of his job but the sentiment was there and Pete and I were glad to receive it.

Ann Annis

Letter from Gordon Brown

10 DOWNING STREET
LONDON SW1A 2AA

THE PRIME MINISTER

Dear Ms Annis,

I and Sarah have been so saddened to hear of Simon's death in Afghanistan and want to offer you and your family my sincere condolences for your sad loss. I know that nothing will ever fill the gap left by Simon's loss but I hope that, over time, you will find some comfort in his incredible courage and bravery, in the esteem and regard in which all who knew Simon held him, and in his extraordinary

Butterflies and Feathers

to his country. Simon will never be forgotten by all of us who knew the commitment and dedication he showed.

The thoughts of Sarah and me are with you. Please let me know if there is anything I can do about you and your family.

Yours sincerely
Gordon Brown

Life without Simon 2010

I started to write this biography of Simon in early May 2010. It has been one of the hardest, most upsetting things I have undertaken. Every day I have relived the memories of Simon, from his birth to his death and it affected my sleep, my attitude and manner on a daily basis. Late at night, dreams awoke me with images of Simon on that fateful day. It's such a small book but if I had of written about our beautiful larger than life boy in his entirety, I would be writing indefinitely.

Since his death, we have a different outlook on life, we have made new, helpful, true friends but we have also seen that death can bring heartless, soulless people who are wrapped up in their own lives. Life is now a plod, before we had a zest for life. Our destinies are set in place from the moment of birth, I believe this now and we are destined to follow a route, whether it takes us into old age or not. Nothing changes this, hindsight is a wonderful word, if only we knew when to follow and take heed of it or ignore it.

When something disastrous happens, like the loss of our child, we feel guilt in everything we do in life without him. The 12 months following Simon's death, our words were always, "this time last year Simon was alive" now those words are changed to "what would he be doing now, there's so much he's missing out on?".

People tell us that time heals, how can that be, as the longer we have to endure life without him, the more we miss him. What would he be doing with his life now, would he have left the Army to pursue his love of diving or would he be that great professional poker player he yearned to be?

For his 23rd Birthday this year, all his family and friends went along to the local park, where we lit and released lanterns for him. Each one had a special message written on it, *"Happy Birthday, love and miss you xx"*. My lantern went up high out of sight, just high enough for him to read.

Butterflies and Feathers

We have a Committee now, the **"Simon Annis Appeal"** is up and running and we have held various events, a sponsored walk, a fancy dress pub crawl and discos. Many more events for this year and next are already scheduled to take place and all monies raised will go to the Fusilier Aid Society. If Simon had survived and if he had come back to us with limbs missing, this charity would no doubt have looked after and cared for him.

Hundreds set of to walk the 15 miles in memory of Simon

Ann Annis

Fancy dress pub crawl in memory of Simon

Pete and I hope to do a 170 mile bike ride in June 2011, to say thanks to all who have supported us. I was frightened that Simon's name would have eventually been forgotten, but we have no fear of this happening now. We may only live in a small Community but people are beginning to independently organise their own events for Simon's Appeal. As well as all this, Simon has a Memorial Brick in the new extension of the High School he attended, along with two more in the walls of the Fusilier Museum in Bury. The two "Trees for Life" planted in his name, are growing tall and strong now.

My dream is this, on the approach to Cadishead there is a small roundabout and in the centre of this plot is an art deco sculpture. I would one day like to see a bronze statue of Simon on this spot, a true fitting monument in honour of all the fine young soldiers who gave their lives in Afghanistan. Maybe my dream will come true one day, who knows?

Natalie has achieved her dream and she started university in September, Simon would have been so pleased and proud of her, she knows this and that has been her inspiration to succeed. The letters Simon told me he was going to write, the letters that were to remain unopened unless anything happened to him, never came, maybe he had no time, maybe he couldn't find the words, and maybe he didn't want to tempt fate. I still wait for these and I tell myself that one day they will come through my letter box, having been recovered amongst lost admin files.

The verdict from the Coroner was given as "Unlawful Killing" and what makes this so hard to me is the fact that surely this means murder. We have no closure, if he had been murdered in this country and the offender was brought to justice, we could have faced him and looked into his eyes, but not in this case and this what makes it so hard to accept. Sadly this is the consequence of war and we know this. He loved the Army; he was a proud man who stood tall in his uniform. When he asked us for advice as to whether he should join or not, we told him to "Go for it". On his Passing out Parade, we saw our son as a man with pride in his heart. Time cannot be reversed and God decided his time was up.

We visit Simon each day, we tend his grave, we cut his lawn, we wash his Heroes head stone and make sure that he has fresh flowers we keep his plot fit for a king. We nurtured our son for 22 years and it makes no difference that he's no longer here with us in life, he's here with us in our hearts and in our memories. We will endeavor to care for him in his final resting place until the day finally comes when his dad and I are no longer here. When that time comes it won't matter because we will be with our son again, this time for eternity and when I meet him, I am going to take hold of my beautiful boy and hold him and say those words that he already knows, *"I love you Simon, Mummies Little Soldier"*.

THE END.

Tributes

His Commanding Officer, Lieutenant Colonel Charlie Calder, 2 RRF, said:

"Fusilier Simon Annis was a larger than life character, and a dedicated soldier. Always at the heart of whatever was going on, it was no surprise to me that he died whilst trying to save his mortally wounded Section Commander. He should be seen as a shining example to the nation of what selfless commitment really means.

Lieutenant Colonel Rob Thomson, Commanding Officer, 2 RIFLES Battle Group, said:

"Fusilier Annis was delightful in addition to being a quality soldier. A huge man, I used to encounter him on my way to breakfast on an almost daily basis and he used to stop me and ask me if I was OK. He had an ever-present grin and used to carry far more than his normal share on patrol. He was always laughing and used to lighten the mood in the darkest of times, often by breaking into particularly tuneless song

His Company Commander, Major Jo Butterfill, Officer Commanding, A Company Group, 2 RRF, said:

"Fusilier Annis was an A Company character from the moment he arrived. A quiet, sometimes unassuming personality, his extraordinary, wry sense of humour and his incredible capacity for shouldering more than his fair share of any task nevertheless made him immensely popular across the ranks. If the job of the infantryman is sometimes simply to endure, then Fusilier Annis had that ability, and then some.

"Unshakable by anything the Army or the enemy could throw at him, he was rock-solid under both fire and the privations of operational life, and never to be found without a smile on his face. It was absolutely typical of the man that he died in the attempt to extract a wounded friend from danger. We have lost a truly excellent soldier, and a staunch comrade; the company is immeasurably poorer for his passing.

Lieutenant Alan Williamson, Platoon Commander, 3 Platoon, A Company, 2 RRF, attached to 2 RIFLES, said:

"How do I sum up Fusilier Annis in just a few short words? Cheeky would be an understatement, the life and soul of the platoon would not be too far from the truth. During our darkest days out here in Sangin Fusilier Annis has been there to lighten the mood and pick up morale. The man was a delight. Whether it be his jokes and banter or his spontaneous outbreak into song he could always make you smile and forget your troubles - how we could do with him now.

"Fusilier Annis was no joker when the chips were down! He was fiercely competent with his LMG [Light Machine Gun], bragging that he was the 'best gunner in battalion', a statement not far from the truth. He was a soldier who was always there for his friends and commanders, never too busy to stop and talk; he has touched a lot of hearts within the Battle Group. I spent three weeks scuba diving in Belize with Fusilier Annis a year ago and he was the centre of attention for the entire trip. On his 21st birthday night out in San Pedro he even managed to befriend some American tourists and convinced them to buy him drinks for most of the night, such was the personality of the man.

"Fusilier Annis was a man with a big heart and a bright future; he was a real people person. It's fitting that he died trying to save his friend, right at the front of the CASEVAC [casualty evacuation] party. I shall miss Fusilier Annis and his quirky sense of humour, his mischievous ways and his appalling singing! My thoughts and prayers are with his family now during these darkest of days."

Corporal Paul Whiting, Section Commander, 3rd Battalion The Yorkshire Regiment, said:

"Fusilier Annis was a character, the little time I knew him, he would always make you smile, whatever the situation. He was another legend of the platoon, if not *the* legend. He was great and very professional. I'm just sorry he won't be able to live out his dreams of becoming a pro poker player. Rest in peace buddy."

Corporal Dan Henderson, 9 Platoon, C Company, said:

"I was Simon's Corporal when he was in training at ITC Catterick. I got to know him very well. He was the light in the section, he had a cheekiness that only he could get away with. No matter how hard things were, Simon could bring a smile to people's faces. Simon was very caring and full of joy, the world is a lesser place without him."

Lance Corporal Nike Thomas, 10 Platoon, C Company, said:

"Simon was one of the funniest lads I have ever met. I was in A Company with him in Cyprus, we would always go out for a few beers together and he would ensure that every night would be memorable. My thoughts go out to all his family.

Fusilier Tom Swann, 3 Platoon, A Company, said:

"Si was one of those blokes you couldn't help but love. He was always smiling, and he was one of the few people who could cheer you up. Whether it was with his snide comments, stupid songs or his atrocious beat boxing. He was always the first to complain about things, but when out on the ground he was fearless, always the first to return fire in contact. He knew when to draw the line and always got the job done. The bloke was an absolute legend, the platoon, company and battalion has lost a true friend. Our thoughts now turn to his family. Our deepest sympathies go out to them. Miss ya mate x."

Lieutenant Colonel Charlie Calder, Commanding Officer 2 RRF

"Fusilier Simon Annis was a larger than life character, and a dedicated soldier. Always at the heart of whatever was going on, it was no surprise to me that he died whilst trying to save his mortally wounded Section Commander. He should be seen as a shining example to the nation of what selfless commitment really means."

Fusilier James Burke, 3 Platoon, A Company, said:

"Simon Annis was one of my best mates. We got to battalion at roughly the same time and have spent all three-and-a-half years in 1 Platoon and now 3 Platoon. Annis was a pain in the arse at times, but I wouldn't have changed him for any other way. Reading your eulogy at your vigil service was one of the hardest things I've ever done, but one of the proudest, telling everybody how awesome a friend you were and how much you meant to me and the 3 Platoon lads. The good guys always die young and that's an understatement for you mate. Been a pleasure mate and I'm sure you'll always be watching over us, keeping us safe. Gone but not forgotten Si!"

Fusilier John Jones, 3 Platoon, A Company, said:

"Si was a good friend of mine, I spoke to him now and then in Hounslow and he made me laugh back then, but it wasn't till we came on tour that I started to know him a lot more. He was always morale for the section and, even if he did wind everyone up now and then, he could always take it when the joke was on him. He was a big fan of poker and always loved taking money off us when we lost. Well, rest in peace my friend, and I'll never forget you or the good times we had. Specky."

Fusilier Jay Connolly, 3 Platoon, A Company, said:

"Si was an awesome soldier and a very loyal friend. If I was to describe Annis in one word, that word would be 'legend'; he would always know how to make you smile, however bad you felt.

Fusilier Andrew Evans, 3 Platoon, A Company, said:

"Si was a person that everyone liked, he had a heart of gold and never had a bad thing to say about anyone, unless it was banter, which he gave out as well as took. He always had a smile on his face and had a way of putting a smile on everyone else's face, no matter how bad things were.

"As a soldier, he knew when to be the joker and when to be a soldier, which he did extremely well. He could be given any task, which he would always do, and smiling whilst doing it. He will always be missed but never replaced; all our thoughts now go to his family."

Fusilier Adam Gregg, 2 Platoon, A Company, said:

"I can't think of many words to describe his sense of humour, which everyone knows was second-to-none, but if I was to describe him as a soldier and a friend, the list is endless. He was honourable, loyal, brave, honest and a true hero, one in a million, just a few that could describe this true hero. He was a true Fusilier and no-one could have asked more of him. My thoughts are with his family and friends."

Fusilier Craig Ashwell, 2 Platoon, A Company, said:

"I've had the privilege to have known Simon for about three years since he first rocked up to battalion in Cyprus. In the time that I've known him he always put a smile on my face. Some of the stuff he would come out with was unbelievable - put it this way, there was never a dull moment with him. He was definitely the joker of the company. He made a lot of friends with his time spent in A Company, you couldn't do anything but love the guy but that was just typical of his nature and the way he did things.

"I'm not just speaking for myself but for the whole of A Company, he will be sorely missed and I still can't believe he's gone but I know he will be watching over us all for the duration of our time left in Afghanistan. My heart and sincere condolences go out to his loving family and to all whom have known him. Goodbye my friend, RIP."

Fusilier Lawrie Stevenson, 2 Platoon, A Company, said:

"Since the start Annis was one of those characters who always made you laugh and we all loved him when he arrived at battalion. In Cyprus I got the privilege to know Annis quite well, he had the ability to make anyone laugh with his dry sense of humour and I'm sure that right now he is watching over the company and most importantly his family. Farewell mate you will always be remembered."

Fusilier Jonathan Hooley, 2 Platoon, A Company, said:

"Good friend and a brilliant soldier. He was laid back and always had a smile on his face no matter what. Annis kept spirits high and he was always there to listen and give a helping hand. He would put others' needs first. He was a brilliant man full of life and will be sorely missed."

Fusilier Ryan Hyndman, 2 Platoon, A Company, said:

"There are so many words that could describe Annis; that's the sort of person he was, full of character. He was one of the friendliest people to meet in this battalion and I am privileged to be one of his many friends. His sense of humour was pure morale and he always made me and the lads laugh. He had this cheeky way about him that you just had to admire. It's a massive loss to this battalion and regiment. He is in all of our thoughts and our hearts and I can only offer my deepest sympathy to his family."

Fusilier Daniel Swales, 9 Platoon, C Company, said:

"Simon and I first met on a diving expedition. He was a very good diver and was always cracking jokes, messing around and had a smile on his face. He was the life of the group and I will truly miss him."

From all the men at Patrol Base Woqab:

"Fallen but not forgotten. Good memories of another great man and… Once a Fusilier always a Fusilier."